GIFTS ANYTIME

GIFTS ANYTIME

HOW TO FIND THE PERFECT PRESENT FOR ANY OCCASION

Leah Ingram

ASJA Press
New York Lincoln Shanghai

Gifts Anytime
How to Find the Perfect Present for Any Occasion

Copyright © 2002, 2005 by Leah Ingram

ASJA Press
an imprint of iUniverse, Inc.

iUniverse books may be ordered through booksellers or by contacting:

iUniverse
2021 Pine Lake Road, Suite 100
Lincoln, NE 68512
www.iuniverse.com
1-800-Authors (1-800-288-4677)

Originally published by Contemporary Books
Originally published as You Shouldn't Have!

ISBN-13: 978-0-595-33621-0 (pbk)
ISBN-13: 978-0-595-80105-3 (cloth)
ISBN-10: 0-595-33621-3 (pbk)
ISBN-10: 0-595-80105-6 (cloth)

Printed in the United States of America

CONTENTS

ACKNOWLEDGMENTS

I love everything having to do with gift giving. I love shopping for gifts, I love receiving gifts, and I even enjoy writing thank-you notes to those who have given me gifts. I don't think I would have developed my love, or expertise, had it not been for my family, who have always been generous with gifts to me—especially my mother, Judy Ingram, and my husband, William Behre. In addition, my children, Jane and Anne, have given me a newfound appreciation for kids' gifts—and been the inspiration for many gifts I've given others, especially their grandparents.

Thanks also to the friends I've made through membership in the American Society of Journalists and Authors and on Freelance Success. Many of you have shared stories of wonderful gifts you've given and received, and without your spirited anecdotes, parts of this book would not have come to life.

Introduction

Gift giving is something you face everyday and throughout your life—from the holiday present you gave your long-ago first-grade teacher to the recent "thanks for the business" gift you might have given to a client. My daughter Jane was less than a year old when she gave her first gift, albeit with my help. It was a T-shirt for her dad that featured Jane's footprints and on which we'd written, "My daddy lets me walk all over him." Jane and I made it together (OK, I painted the bottoms of Jane's feet with fabric paint and helped her to "walk" across the shirt), and we gave it to my husband for Father's Day.

The gift itself took less than ten minutes to make, and probably less than $10 for supplies, but it was a gift he truly loved and still loves: it was from his daughter and his wife, it had great sentiment attached to it, and it was something that—I believed—a T-shirt lover such as my husband would really appreciate. I know I was right because he still proudly wears that shirt nearly ten years later—and to this day, he reminds me of the shirt's specific laundering instructions (no bleach, not too long in the dryer) because he wants it to last for a long time.

In my opinion, this simple gift has the elements that make it a great gift: it was geared toward the recipient's likes (he's a world-class T-shirt guy), and it had personal meaning for him (what dad wouldn't love something that his child helped to make, especially on his first Father's Day?). Of course, it's easy for me to analyze my own performance in this regard, since I'm considered to be a gift expert. What I hope to do through "Gifts Anytime" is help you to become a great gift giver, too. Obviously, you're ready for some help, or you wouldn't be reading this book.

Rules of Gift Giving

Now, I know how stressful giving a gift can be for most, particularly when you consider how many gifts you could potentially give each year. According to a recent survey the average American buys forty-seven gifts annually! That's nearly one gift per week each year. If you enjoy gift giving as I do, you may give many more gifts than that, especially if you count the bottle of wine or the box of dessert you brought with you to your friend's home the last time you were invited over for dinner. Technically, the wine and desserts count as a hostess gift and therefore contribute to your overall annual gift tally.

Given all of this gift giving that's going on, it would seem that sooner or later you'd run out of gift ideas. However, that doesn't have to be the case. There are five basic rules that I believe can be applied to any gift-giving situation and when you follow these rules, your gift giving will get a lot easier. I mention these rules repeatedly throughout the book. They are:

* Know the Occasion and Your Recipient
* Consider Your Budget
* Whenever Possible, Personalize the Gifts
* Gather Gift Intelligence Year Round
* Don't Try to Reinvent the Wheel

Let me explain how each of these rules work.

Know the Occasion and Your Recipient

You wouldn't buy your boss lingerie to congratulate her on her promotion, nor would you buy your betrothed a silver pen on Valentine's Day. But switch the situations, and the gifts make perfect sense. It may seem utterly obvious that lingerie doesn't mix with the office—but you would be surprised: Many, many people don't stop to think about the occasion for which they're giving a gift, as well as the recipient, before they make a purchase.

Do your homework before you start shopping. Ask questions of those who've gone before you in giving a gift to this person—whether it's a personal gift to a family member or something for a colleague. Find out what is and isn't part of the culture in your social setting or work environment. Prompt people for examples of presents that have brought down the house in the past—and ones that bombed so miserably that you'll know to avoid them at all costs. Then, once you have a good sense of the dos and don'ts for the gift-giving situation, you can start shopping with confidence.

Consider Your Budget

Most people assume that you always have to break your budget when it comes to buying gifts, especially around the holidays, but that simply isn't true. The fact that your brother makes a million dollars on Wall Street doesn't mean that you need to spend megabucks on gifts for him. You shouldn't ever feel that you must equate the value of your gift to the recipient's household income or give a gift that mimics the amount that you think someone has spent on your in the past. Instead, you should gear your gift toward your own budget and what feels right to you. For example, you may find the perfect present for your mother on eBay or at a discount store like Marshall's or TJ Maxx. However, just because you can get the gift at a dirt-cheap price doesn't mean you shouldn't buy it. If you know your mom is going to love it, forget how much you paid for it and just buy it.

You should never come away from any gift-giving situation feeling that you spent too much or that some external forces had pressured you into spending more than you wanted. Decide ahead of time approximately how much you would like to spend on the gift, look for a gift you believe the recipient will love, and do your best not to veer from your budget.

Whenever Possible, Personalize the Gift

When I say you should "personalize" a gift, I'm not saying pay extra to have that scarf monogrammed, although monogrammed gifts make a wonderful impression. The point here is to choose a gift that will feel personal to the recipient—because, ideally, it is related to a favorite hobby or activity that this person enjoys. In other words you should think about what that person likes to do in his or her free time and then use this information to guide your gift choice.

One year, my husband gave me a new camera for a Christmas present. You may think that a camera is a ho-hum gift, but I certainly wasn't yawning when I opened it. I've always been a bit of a shutterbug. I was the photo editor of my high school yearbook, spent hours in the darkroom at college, and once worked as a freelance photographer in New York City. However, after we had kids, it was impossible to drag around all of my professional equipment to take impromptu pictures, so I stopped taking pictures altogether. My husband knew how much I missed this activity. He also knew that buying me a pocket-sized digital camera that had all the features of my professional equipment but without the bulk was the perfect gift for me. And it absolutely was.

Gather Gift Intelligence Year Round

For most people gift buying becomes their top priority around Thanksgiving, when all media go into holiday mode and all you can think about is shop, shop, and shop. Sure, you probably have other times throughout the year when you might feel some gift-giving pressure, such as Mother's or Father's Day, or if you're the parent of a young child, at the end of the school year. (That would be for teacher gifts, in case you were wondering.)

One way to avoid feeling completely stressed out whenever you are in the market for a gift is this: do not leave the thinking about the gift until the last minute. I'm a big fan of gathering gift intelligence all year round, which means that you're always alert for gift clues or hints that people may drop on purpose or tell you inadvertently. Let me tell you how this works.

Two years ago I was attending the open school night at my daughters' elementary school, which traditionally occurs in September. I'd just sat down at my older daughter's desk when her then second grade teacher started talking about her daily routine. Her mission in telling us about what she does before and after school was to help parents know when they would have the best time reaching her on email or the phone. For me, though, it was a bright beacon for the perfect gift to give this teacher at the holidays.

In discussing her daily routine, the teacher mentioned that every day after school she went to our local coffee shop to grade papers. I knew that if I got her a gift certificate to that coffee shop as her holiday gift, she would definitely appreciate it and, more importantly, use it, which I know she did—she sent me one of the most heartfelt thank-you notes I've ever received.

Another example of gift intelligence happened recently with my husband. We had invited some friends over for dinner and we were all sitting around the table discussing our favorite movies. My husband happened to mention his favorite movie (which I knew) and how every time he's in the store he means to buy it for himself on DVD (which I didn't know). Guess what my husband is getting for his birthday this year? You got it—that favorite movie on DVD!

Don't Reinvent the Wheel

Sometimes out of pure luck, you hit the gift-giving jackpot. You give your mother-in-law a gift that you figured she'd like, and instead of just liking it, she's in seventh heaven. Not only does she tell everyone who'll listen what a swell gift you gave her, but also she continues to talk about how much she likes that gift months later. If this has happened to you on a certain occasion, then I say, "Don't mess with success." That is, if a certain kind of gift worked in the past for a certain person, give it again. And again. There's no reason you should tax yourself at each birthday or holiday by trying to reinvent the gift-giving wheel.

Of course, if that winning gift is the pearl necklace you gave your sister for her birthday last year, logically you wouldn't give her another pearl necklace this year. But you can give her accessories to go along with the necklace, such as matching earrings, a pearl pin, or even a new jewelry box. All of these gift ideas go along the theme of that successful gift, and by doing so, you're assured to continue to give your sister a gift she loves.

The next time you find yourself in need of a gift—but stumped as to what to buy—keep these five tips in mind. I promise that they'll help you find a great gift for anyone on your gift-giving list.

GIFTS ANYTIME

❧ 1 ❦

COMMON GIFT-GIVING QUESTIONS

It's a familiar pattern: you need to buy a gift but you don't know where to start. Other times, you think you should send a present, but you're not sure. This chapter presents a list of frequently asked questions (or FAQs, in computer-speak) that I've collected on the subject of gift giving. They range from general queries to specific quandaries, and I hope the answers will help make all of your gift-giving decisions easier.

Gift-Giving FAQs

Q: Is it OK to give the same gift to someone year after year?
A: If you've found a gift that you know the person enjoyed getting (because he or she told you so), why mess with success? I'm a big believer in sticking with gifts that work and are well received. Gift giving can get out of control and can become way too stressful if you have to reinvent the wheel, so to speak, each year when finding gifts for holidays and birthdays.

Gift Giving FYI

When it comes to wrapping gifts, Americans use a lot of wrapping paper—nearly seven regular-sized rolls for holiday gifts alone, according to a new survey by 3M, the makers of Scotch brand tapes. However, when we run out of wrapping paper, we don't all run to the store; Americans tend to complete the gift-wrapping job with whatever they find around the house. According to the same 3M survey, here are some of the gift-wrapping alternatives we use, as well as the percentage of people who turn to these offbeat wrapping resources. Next time you run short of paper, you might consider using:

paper or plastic bags	28%
newsprint	24%
tissue paper	15%
comics	14%
plastic wrap	6%
aluminum foil	5%
discarded yellow pages	1%

Of course, this rule applies only when you're certain that the recipients genuinely like what you gave them. So, ask—and tell them to be honest with you. This lets people know that you care enough to give them the best gift. If your last gift didn't bowl them over, ask what they would like instead. Solicit a couple of ideas, make note of them, and then choose one of these items for the next occasion.

As always, stick with suggestions that fall within your price range. If your brother tells you that what he'd really like is a brand-new Hummer, that's surely a bit much to come through with. However, you could give him the Matchbox version as a gift. Then you could let him know, in an accompanying note, how much you wished that you had unlimited income to buy him the real thing and how you hope he'll appreciate the scaled-down version instead.

Q: Is it ever OK to give cash as a gift?
A: I believe cash, or its equivalent in the form of a gift certificate or gift card, is appropriate in many situations. I don't think that you shouldn't feel awkward about the practice of giving cash as a gift, as long as you know that your doing so won't be taken the wrong way, such as giving it to someone at work who may misconstrue your generosity as a bribe.

My children's grandparents often send a crisp $5 or $10 bill for the kids' birthdays or as part of their Christmas gifts, and my girls love getting "real" money that they can spend for themselves. Religious celebrations such as bar mitzvahs are also times when you should have no qualms about giving cash, as are graduations from high school or college. And if cash gifts are acceptable in your social circle as wedding gifts (as they are on the East Coast where I grew up), by all means write the bride and groom a check.

Many times you can give the cash equivalent as a gift. You can buy a savings bond upon the birth of a child, or a gift certificate from a home-decor or hardware retailer for a housewarming. For example, my mother gave my husband and me two $100 The Home Depot gift cards when we moved into our house. They were one of the most practical and used housewarming gifts we received.

If you want to get a little creative with your money gift, why not package it in a fun container? For instance, if you want to give money to a newly married couple or new home owners, place it in a watering can and include a card that says you hope this gift will help them sow the seeds of a happy life together—or something like that. (Make sure you're clear to the recipients that there is something inside the watering can before they put it to use.) For a kid going off to college, you can put the money in a take-out food container (available at craft stores or on eBay in a variety of colors), and write a card that says you hope the student will use this money to help treat himself to a meal on the nights when the dining hall just won't do. Have some fun with the packaging, and you'll end up giving a practical gift that will be fondly remembered.

Q: What are some good alternatives to taking a bottle of wine as a hostess gift when you are invited to someone's house for dinner?
A: I think a bottle of wine is always welcomed when you're invited for dinner— that is, unless you know that the hosts have an alcohol dependency. Then, it would be in bad taste. You'll hear me saying this a lot: there's no reason to reinvent the wheel each time you must give someone a gift, including taking something for dinner. My friends know that I love white wine, so if they show up with a bottle of Pinot Grigio (my favorite) each time we invite them to dinner, I'm in heaven. I don't expect them to change what they bring, and I'm glad my friends are comfortable coming to dinner with the same wine each time.

❧ The Best Gift I Ever Got ❧

My daughter has a genetic disease that was diagnosed when she was two. Before we knew what was wrong with her, she was very sick, and my husband and I spent a lot of time at the hospital and away from home. One of the best gifts we received arrived shortly after all three of us came home: my coworkers, who had been wonderfully supportive throughout this ordeal, arranged to have dinner delivered to our apartment from our favorite restaurant—not only the first night we were home, but for a full week. I never remember food tasting so good as it did that first night. I truly appreciated this gift.

Jeanne, New York

However, if for some reason you feel you must take something different to
dinner every once and awhile, why not try a twist on the bottle-of-wine approach
and instead take a bottle of sparkling cider? This beverage is available in abun-
dance during the fall. Or how about taking an appetizer or a dessert? There is a
French bakery in our town called C'est La Vie that is truly *magnifique* and makes
sublime desserts: Whenever we go to someone's house for dinner, if we're not taking wine, we visit this shop and pick up a scrumptious pear tart or some
meringue cookies. Another good food gift to bring along is a box of chocolates.
I've never had anyone turn me away when I show up with this confection.

You can also put together a gift basket of whole coffee beans or various coffee
flavors, along with festive mugs, and present them as your hostess gift. Or you
can give spa goodies, like lotions, candles and bath salts, which encourage the
hostess to take time for herself, after her dinner party, and indulge in some well-
deserved relaxation.

The Best All-Occasion Gifts

One of the most awkward situations to find yourself in is needing to give a last-minute
gift but not having anything on hand that qualifies. You can avoid this fate by keeping a
treasure trove of all-occasion gifts at your home at all times in what I appropriately call a
gift closet. The best way to keep your gift closet stocked is by purchasing potential gift
items all year long, especially when you see them on sale at your favorite store. And the
key is to stock up on gifts that anyone could enjoy, including picture frames, note cards
and gift cards.

Recently, I was shopping for back-to-school supplies at Staples when what to my wondering eyes should appear but a score of cute plastic picture frames in vibrant hues of
green apple, bubble gum, and grape. Besides being eye-catching, they'd been marked

down to less than two bucks each. Needless to say, I bought all twenty of them, and now I'm set for any gift "emergency" for which a colorful picture frame is appropriate.

The clearance aisle at your favorite retailer isn't the only place to seek out bargains. You can usually get some good buys at an outlet store, and even deep discounts if you time it right. Last month, my local Van Heusen outlet had men's ties on sale for $9, a tempting deal. And last year, Nordstrom Rack (the outlet version of Nordstrom department store) had notepaper with whimsical watercolor drawings on sale for about $2 per pack of eight. You can be sure I racked up a bunch. If you live near an outlet center, make it a practice to check in often so that you can catch the specials.

Gift cards and gift certificates can also serve their turn as last-minute gifts. Stores, businesses, and even restaurants sometimes will offer customers a gift card or certificate in a moderate denomination as an incentive to come back in the near future, and this is an excellent (and free) way of picking up one or more for your trove. Case in point: My family and I recently had lunch at the Rainforest Cafe. Along with our bill came a discount coupon for the Rainforest Store, which is adjacent to the Cafe. If we spent a certain amount of money in the store, we would receive two $25 gift certificates to the restaurant. Shopping trips to stores such as Target and Old Navy yielded similar benefits: because we spent a certain amount in those stores that day, we received $10 gift cards gratis.

As you can see, it's easy to be prepared even when you're taken by surprise, Stock up on the following great all-occasion gifts, and you won't get caught holding the bag:

1. Picture frames
2. Notepaper
3. Vases
4. Bath products
5. Kids' art supplies
6. Men's ties
7. Gift cards or certificates from local stores or businesses
8. High-end pens
9. Packages of golf balls and tees
10. Portable tool kits (such as a Swiss Army knife or Leatherman multi-purpose tool)

Q: I have a friend whose family earns a lot more than mine does, and she's always giving me extravagant gifts that I know cost a lot. I always feel bad when I give her something, because I'm afraid she'll look down on me and my gift for not meeting her standards. Should I blow my budget and buy her something really extravagant, too?
A: If this person who gives you such expensive gifts each year is a really good friend, I doubt she even stops to consider the value of the gifts you give her. I'm

sure she's thrilled that you and she are close enough to exchange gifts and simply appreciates the sentiment with which the gifts are given. And that's the way gift giving should be. Now, if the person does comment on the value of the gift or where you got it, then maybe you need to reconsider whether you want to be exchanging gifts with this person at all. But that's a judgment call on your part.

As I said in the Introduction, one of my rules is that you should never take the recipient's salary into account when buying a gift. If someone always buys you something from an upscale store, you shouldn't feel compelled to do your shopping there as well. Rather, you should give something that suits your own budget and about which you feel good giving. That means that if you find the perfect present for your girlfriend at a bargain price on eBay or at a store like Marshall's, by all means buy it for her.

Q: How do I handle gift-giving occasions when I'm no longer close to someone? Do I still need to send gifts each birthday or holiday?
A: No. It is normal for friendships to wax and wane, and for the sake of your financial stability and your own sanity, you need to readdress your gift list each year. Figure out the people to whom you no longer want to send gifts, for whatever reason that may be, and either remove them from your list completely or "wean" them off. In the latter case, instead of sending a gift for a birthday or holiday, send a card with a personal note in it. See if they respond in kind at your birthday or at Christmas. If they don't, then the following year, you can delete them entirely. If you don't hear from people at traditional occasions such as a birthday or the holidays, you have to accept that the friendship has run its course and you need to let it go. However, if it feels right to continue sending a greeting at the holidays, by all means do so. Just don't make yourself crazy by buying and sending gifts to someone you no longer communicate with regularly.

Here's a model you can follow to keep yourself organized so that you're not wasting money on cards or gifts for people from whom you've grown apart over time. Each December, between Christmas and New Year's, I'll set aside an afternoon to enter the birthdays and anniversaries of my friends and family members and their kids into my Palm Pilot. I write the person's name on the date of his or her birthday or anniversary and, if I have the information, how old the person will be or what anniversary it is. Then throughout the year on a biweekly basis, I look through the coming weeks to see if there are any birthdays for which I need to send cards and/or gifts. Since I stock up on birthday cards (I save money by buying when the price is right and always have cards on hand), I usually only have to open a filing cabinet drawer to get a card. If I'm sending a gift, and if I don't want to raid the stash in my gift closet, I'll plan to do the necessary shopping and shipping well in advance.

But back to the notion of whether or not you should buy gifts for those you're no longer close to. Over the years, I've accepted that the roster of people whose birthdays or anniversaries I'd previously jotted in my calendar may not stay the same. If we no longer stay in touch, I don't feel the need to commemorate special occasions with a gift or a card. And when I do my yearly review of my roster, I can decide if it's time to take that person's name of my list and not bother to enter his or her birthday or anniversary information into my Palm.

For example, when my husband was attending graduate school, we lived in university family housing, which was actually like a glorified army barracks. Because of the tight quarters there, we couldn't help but become close with the families who lived nearby. All of our children played together, and we would exchange cards and gifts on birthdays and holidays. When, after graduate school, members of the informal group slowly started moving away and taking jobs in different parts of the country, we kept up with the gift exchange for the first year or two. Then it transitioned to just cards. Now we may send an occasional E-mail message just to say "Hello," and each year we exchange holiday greetings. However, I no longer write the names and birthdays of these long-ago friends and their children in my calendar because the friendships have simply run their course, and I'm OK with that. Some of them have even stopped sending holiday greetings, and I'm OK with that, too.

Are you feeling weighed down by the gift buying and card sending that you're saddled with at each birthday and holiday? If so, then I say that's a sign that you need to re-evaluate the state of your friendships and use the exercise I described above by doing an annual audit of your friendships to see if it still makes sense for you to send gifts to all of these people or whether you should just start sending cards. However, if there are people who have never reciprocated or even acknowledged your generosity, you may want to stop sending them anything at all.

Would You Like That Gift-Wrapped?

If you ever stressed out about how to wrap a certain gift, imagine what people throughout history had to confront when presenting the following very large tokens:

- In 1912, Japan presented the then first lady Helen Herron Taft with more than three thousand cherry trees of twelve varieties to be planted in Washington, D.C.'s tidal basin. Those trees still stand today and are the central feature of Washington's famous Cherry Blossom Festival.

- Muslim emperor Shah Jahan of India had the Taj Majal built as a gift for his wife, Queen Mumtaz Majal. It is made entirely of white marble. It took twenty-two years to complete—unfortunately, Queen Majal died before it was done.
- France gave the American people the Statue of Liberty as a gift. Frédéric-Auguste Bartholdi designed and presented it in 1886. In order for it to get here, though, it had to be dismantled piece by piece, shipped in large crates to New York, and then reassembled on Liberty Island in New York Harbor.

Q: Is it ever inappropriate to send a gift when you find out that someone is sick or in the hospital? What about when someone dies?

A: For some reason, people are often hesitant to acknowledge when bad things happen in someone's life. I don't know if they think that it's bad manners or bad luck to discuss illness or death, but in my opinion, it's extremely bad manners not to at least acknowledge that something has happened. At a minimum, you should send a handwritten note to the sick person or the survivor to say that you're thinking of him or her and that you send your best wishes. You don't have to gush or go on and on about how sorry you are. A few brief but heartfelt lines are all that's necessary.

That's exactly what I did recently when I found out that a friend had suffered a miscarriage. I wrote a three-line note to tell her that while I had no idea what she and her husband must be going through, I wanted her to know that I was thinking of them. I hope that the note provided her with some comfort during that very difficult time.

Most people tend to send flowers when someone is sick or recovering from the death of a loved one. Flowers are a fine all-occasion gift (even if the occasion is one steeped in sadness), but sometimes you want your gift to be more than pretty. For these times, if you give something that will make the person's life easier during the recovery—such as food or assistance—you'll have given something truly special.

For instance, a thoughtful gift to send to someone who has just returned home from a hospital stay or a funeral is a few days' worth of homemade frozen meals. Package them in serving-size containers so that they can be popped into the microwave for an easy-to-fix, hot repast. If time or distance won't allow you to prepare and deliver the meals yourself, have a local restaurant or catering company send some from its menu.

Another gift that will help make life easier is to arrange for a cleaning service to visit the person's home on a regular basis. That way, housecleaning will be one less chore for your friend to worry about. One caveat to this suggestion: There are certain people for whom cleaning is therapeutic, and offering to have someone else perform the act may be seen as an intrusion. If you suspect this person is a cleaning-equals-therapy type, go with something else, such as food.

For a family with small children, a wonderful gift is the offer of free baby-sitting. You can suggest transporting the children to your own home to give the recovering person some quiet time, or just taking the kids out to lunch and a movie during the weekend. If you have a network of like-minded friends, belong to a playgroup, or are involved in a baby-sitting co-op, you can arrange it so that the family in need has enough babysitters lined up for days or weeks.

Whichever you choose, it will be a gift that is much appreciated.

❧ 2 ❧

A BABY IS BORN

Becoming a parent is one of the most exciting events in a person's life—whether the baby arrives via adoption or pregnancy and childbirth. I have two children, and I can't imagine what life would be like without my daughters. What helped me get into the spirit of becoming a mother with each child's birth were the wonderful gifts that family and friends bestowed on my husband, Bill, and me during those very long nine months of gestation. I loved that people close to us didn't wait until our little bundle of joy arrived to give us gifts—although many showered us with good tidings after the births as well.

If you learn that a friend, family member, or work colleague is pregnant—and you know she's sharing the good news publicly—then feel free to give her a gift right away to celebrate the happy news. Late in my pregnancy with my first daughter, an ultrasound confirmed that Jane would be a Jane and not a John. We shared the news with our neighbors, with whom we'd grown close. The next day, they came by to deliver a small wrapped box, which contained a tiny porcelain statue of an angel holding a sign that said "It's a girl." That figurine probably cost no more than $5, but it meant a million bucks to us because it was the first time someone had memorialized that we were going to have a daughter. I treasure that statue, and it became a fixture in the nursery after Jane was born and then in the room she shared with her sister, Anne, after she came along. Today, Jane is in elementary school, and the angel still holds a place of honor along with other prized possessions in her bedroom.

The Gift of Literature

Another class of while-you're-pregnant gifts that Bill and I received—and which I heartily recommend—is books on becoming a parent. One of our favorites was a compilation of the comic strip "Baby Blues," which chronicles the ups and downs of being a parent. This book, called *I Saw Elvis in My Ultrasound,* is all about the hilarious antics of preparing for baby number two, and it was an ideal gift when I was pregnant with our second daughter.

❧ *The Best Gift I Ever Got* ❧

At my baby shower, my best friend gave me a beautiful, black-and-white cotton kimono to wear when I was nursing (or any time, just to be comfortable). What was so striking about this was that all the other gifts were for the baby, but this one was for me. A number of years later, I did something similar for a friend having a baby shower: I gave her luxurious body creams and shampoos instead of baby T-shirts and booties. She loved the gift for the same reason I loved the kimono.

Susan, New York

Gift Giving FYI

Many families like to keep a copy of the newspaper from the day their children were born. If you live far away from a friend or relative who just had a baby, why not send a copy of your local paper from the big day? It will provide a different perspective on that day's news and add to that child's collection of mementos from his or her "birth" day.

Besides giving us books we could enjoy together, some friends purchased books with just one of us in mind. Bill received several humorous books from friends and family on becoming a father, and I got similar books on becoming a mother. One of my favorites was (and still is) Anne Lamott's *Operating Instructions.*

Books for the Mother-to-Be

To date, I've probably read *Operating Instructions* at least five times yet I've only had two children. The reason I continue to read this book again and again is not only because of its topic—becoming a mother—but because it's so beautifully written. (You may have seen Lamott's writing on Salon.com.)

In this pint-size paperback, you become immersed in Lamott's struggle during her son's first year of life as she adapts not only to becoming a parent but a single parent at that. You get the lowdown on being up all night, breastfeeding hits and misses, and how it is that new mothers sometimes go for days without bathing. Some sections are laugh-out-loud funny; other parts are so poignant that you can't help but be moved. This book was so instrumental in helping me accept that being a parent is a crazy combination of flawed and funny moments that it is now my standard "congratulations on becoming pregnant" gift. I usually send a copy as soon as someone I know well and who will appreciate this book announces she's expecting.

❧ The Best Gift I Ever Got ❦

After my third child was born, a friend brought over a gift, which I assumed would be some kind of clothing or toy for the baby. Imagine how delighted I was when I discovered it was a gift for *me:* a basket filled with scented soaps, lotions, and more.

Melanie, Wisconsin

While *Operating Instructions* is my parenting book of choice, plenty of other titles out there would also fill the bill. Is there a book that has meant a lot to you as a parent? If so, send a copy as a gift when someone you care about shares the good news. Remember: new parents—even those welcoming a subsequent child—are ravenous for information on what it's really like to assume the role.

Typically, within days of seeing that little line on the pregnancy test that tells a woman she's with child, she runs to a bookstore to scope out the complete *What to Expect...*series, plus any other titles that seem germane. Then, she usually loads up on subscriptions to parenting magazines so that she'll be 100 percent prepared for the big birth day. You can help her build her library of information through your gift. Here are some off-the-shelf suggestions to consider when purchasing a book as a gift for the expectant parent:

Insert an Inscription

You can add a special touch to a gift of a book by writing a heartfelt inscription inside the cover. If the book has personal meaning to you, mention that in your note.

Give an Autographed Copy

Another way to make your selection more meaningful requires some planning, but if you can pull it off, the gift will be worth the time. Find out if the author of your favorite book for expectant parents is coming to your town or a town near you for a book signing (look for lists of events at the bookstore or in the newspaper or even on the author's personal website). Then, at the signing, buy a stack of those books and have the author autograph each of them. Now, when you give the book as a gift, it will be even more valuable because it bears the author's signature.

❧ *The Best Gift I Ever Gave* ❧

When I was pregnant with number three, my sister was pregnant with her first. Since I couldn't be there for her baby shower, I decided to give her a shower by mail. I had everyone mail me the gifts they intended to give her, then I put them all in a huge box and had her shower delivered to her. Unbeknownst to me, my sister was planning the same thing for me, even though I was having my third child. One day, my friend and her husband dropped by unexpectedly. They came bearing balloons, flowers, gifts, and a cake—all sent courtesy of my sister.

Barb, Kentucky

This is exactly what I did a few years back when Anne Lamott was going to be in my town for a book signing. I bought ten copies of *Operating Instructions* and had Lamott sign her name to each. (I even took along my own dog-eared copy for her to sign as well.) Then, whenever one of my friends announced she was going to have a baby, I sent an author-signed version of the book. Sadly, my supply ran out this year, so I'm keeping my eyes and ears open for future Anne Lamott signings in my area.

Books to Avoid

While I fully endorse giving books about becoming a parent to friends who are about to go down that momentous path, I believe there are two categories of baby books that should be left for the new parents to get for themselves. They are baby-naming books and a child's baby book.

When I was pregnant with my children, Bill and I had a certain criteria for choosing our child's name. We didn't want anyone to influence us in our decision and therefore were particular about the name books we consulted. If anyone had purchased a baby-naming book for us, we would have felt that the person was barging in on a private matter.

Choosing each of our children's baby books was also an intimate experience. Since I was the one who would be the recorder of the events, I wanted to make sure that the book I bought for each of my daughters provided what I knew I wanted: lots of empty space to jot down thoughts or to put keepsakes in, a calendar of momentous occasions, and a height and weight chart for tracking growth. Because I was so particular about what I wanted, it would have been almost impossible for someone to read my mind and buy this kind of book for me. Assuming that other parents will feel the same way, play it safe and leave it up to them to buy the right baby book for their needs.

The Name Game: We Have a Winner

Having anointed me with a then-unique name, my parents could never find anything with the name "Leah" printed on it. I always longed for a "Leah" bicycle license plate, and since I could never find one, I swore I wouldn't subject my children to the same kind of frustration. I promised myself that I would give them simple names so that they would always be able to find stuff with their names on it. So, I christened my daughters Jane and Anne. But in this day and age, when Michaela and Catelyn are the names du jour, searching out items imprinted with "Jane" and "Anne" is about as fruitful as my search for Leah-imprinted items some thirty years ago.

That's why I was thrilled to learn about the NameTrain from Maple Landmark, a toy maker in Middlebury, Vermont. This charming wooden train features an engine and caboose, with the letters of your name in between. (I have the "Leah" version sitting in my office.) The festively colored letters are individual train cars, yielding an endless combination for today's modern names—or, in the case of my daughters, yesterday's classics. At about $30 (more for longer names), this train is just the ticket for babies as well as their older siblings. Maple Landmark also carries a variety of other wooden toys, which you can explore on the website at maplelandmark.com or by call-ing (800) 421-4223.

Books for Baby

Even though as newborns my daughters probably couldn't appreciate the wry humor of *Goodnight, Moon*, we still read them bedtime stories each night. We know that research shows that children reap long-term benefits when their par-ents read to them, even as an infant, so it's never to early to start. (Some parents go as far as reading to the mother's pregnant belly!) That's why giving children's books is always a great gift to give new parents. I know that I enjoyed some of the most meaningful moments as a new parent when I would read aloud to my chil-dren, and more often than not, the books I read were the very ones that people had given as a gift to welcome our children to the world.

I was raised in a home that teemed with books, and I knew from the very beginning that I wanted my children to grow up in the same kind of environment in which reading is revered. So, every book we received to commemorate the birth of our daughters was seen as a loving and thoughtful gift that would, we hoped, contribute to a lifelong love of reading. The books that meant the most were the ones that came with a personal inscription or card that described why the giver had chosen it. I discovered that some of my business colleagues had a softer side when it came to Hans Christian Andersen tales, and I was thrilled when friends shared how much their kids had enjoyed a certain Eric Carle book—and that they were giving it to one of my daughters in hopes that she would enjoy it as much.

❧ The Best Gift I Ever Gave ❦

I recently attended my sister's baby shower. Her gift table was already overflowing with rattles, blankets, and bibs when she got to my gift—a camera. When she opened it and held it up, exclamations of "What a great gift!" and "Why didn't I think of that?" swept the room. I knew that new parents are avid picture-takers, so a camera—film or digital—would be a thoughtful gift that she could use for years to come.

Joanna, New York

❧ *The Best Gift I Ever Got* ❧

My wife and I were in graduate school when our first child was born.
Some friends gave my son and me matching Michigan sweatshirts for
watching football games together. I was deeply touched by the gift—and
amazed at how small his sweatshirt was compared with mine. I dressed
him in that sweatshirt each week until his head got too big to fit inside
the neck. Now a teddy bear in his room sports the sweatshirt.

Bill, Michigan

I try to apply the same thinking when I'm buying a book for a child or to give
an about-to-be new parent. If you have children, what are some of the books that
they've enjoyed flipping through again and again? Are there certain books from
your childhood that have withstood the test of time? These are good thoughts to
keep in mind as you ponder which book to buy for a newborn or his parents.
Most parents will be immensely pleased to add whatever book you settle on to the
child's personal library.

Clothing for Mother and Child

One of the fun things about being pregnant is acquiring an entirely new
wardrobe—for yourself and your baby. In the early months of my pregnancies, I
eagerly perused maternity shops for my new wardrobe, something I knew I needed if I wanted to look and feel good as my pregnancy progressed. It can get awful-
ly expensive to have to buy all this new clothing, which is why a splendid gift for
an expectant mother is maternity clothing you've picked out on her behalf or a
gift certificate to a store that stocks maternity gear so that she can use it to take
herself shopping.

Gift-Giving FAQ

*Q: Do you give a present to someone who is having a second baby? And, if so, should you buy
something of equal value to what you spent on the first kid?*
A: You should send a gift each time someone with whom you're close has a baby—
whether it's the second or seventh. It's really not fair to the child or the family to send a

gift only to the firstborn. The birth (or adoption) of each child comes with a unique set of circumstances worth celebrating, so recognize the good news with a gift.

As far as how much to spend, you can use the gift you bought for the first child as a guideline, but don't jump through hoops. Even though I'm a gift-giving expert, I don't keep a log of what I gave to whom and how much I've spent over the years. If I sent a friend's baby a gift three years ago and now she's had another child, I'm not going to rummage through my old credit card bills to determine exactly how generous I was before. Instead, I'll use my best judgment to find an appropriate gift for that child—and I'll be sure to send along a small gift to the big brother or big sister as well.

Use the Internet

It turns out that the Internet is an almost effortless way to get your itchy hands on super maternity clothes, including certain items that aren't available in brick-and-mortar stores. Best of all, if you're shopping for a friend who lives far away, the Web retailer can wrap the gift for you, enclose a greeting, and deliver the package to your friend's doorstep. Here are two superb sites that I recommend you surf over to when you're in the market for maternity clothes for yourself or a special friend.

Target.com. Like the brick-and-mortar version, what's not to love about Target.com? The site claims to have more than 15,000 items on it—about right when you consider the wide variety of items in the stores. For a long-distance friend who is expecting, be sure to check out Target's maternity wear from either In Due Time or designer Liz Lange, and choose something that can be delivered directly to her. While the selection isn't as varied as what you would find at a maternity-only store, the clothes are fashionable and functional and the prices are just right. Best of all, should your gift selection miss the mark, the recipient can return it, within 90 days and with the shipping receipt, to any of Target's more than 1,300 stores for a full refund.

Gap Maternity. Ubiquitous retailer Gap has delved into the maternity world. On-line at Gap Maternity, part of Gap.com, it's all expectant wear all the time. (Many larger brick-and-mortar Gap stores also have a maternity section, letting you shop in person, if you choose. You can go to Gap.com and use the store locator to see if there is a Gap Maternity shop near you.) If mothers-to-be had their druthers (and unlimited funds alongside), they'd likely be pointing and clicking their way to a new expectant wardrobe compliments of Gap Maternity. Here you'll find fashionable work staples, comfy casual clothes, and even items you'd expect to see at the Gap in your mall, such as boot-cut jeans, but these are made especially for a pregnant woman's expanding waistline. Just looking at these offerings makes me want to be pregnant again. That's why this website is a great place to shop when you want to present your pregnant friends with some new duds. And they'll appreciate that anything you buy them from the Gap Maternity line that doesn't fit, or that they don't like, they can return to a regular Gap retail location or back to the website for free. (All orders come with a prepaid postage sticker.)

Gift Giving FYI

If you want a newborn to have a better chance of growing up a millionaire, give a gift of investing from the National Association of Investors Corporation (NAIC). For $20, plus a one-time $7 setup fee, you can sign a child up for NAIC membership and get a stock-investment program going. Call toll-free (877) ASK-NAIC (275-6242) or visit the better-investing.org website for the skinny.

Clothes for Baby

When a friend or family member is expecting, it's always fun to go shopping for adorable outfits for the little tyke to come. Before I had kids, I delighted in having a reason to check out the children's department of my favorite store and in putting together an ensemble that I imagined would make a baby look like an angel. But then I had kids, and I started to look at children's clothing in a new way.

Clothes became something that you put on babies to keep them warm (or cool, depending on the season), and that was about it. When you needed to pack a diaper bag or grab an outfit in the morning—after not sleeping much the night before—you weren't thinking about fashion but rather function. With countless diaper changes throughout the day, the best clothes were those that offered easy access (read: snaps on the legs). In addition, regardless of whether you were breast-feeding, bottle-feeding, or introducing solids, you were pretty much guaranteed that at least one meal of the day would end up somewhere on your baby's clothes. That meant a lot of dirty laundry and outfit changes. The best clothes were ones that weren't made of white fabric, didn't stain, could withstand multiple trips through the washer and dryer, and offered the aforementioned easy access.

Let me offer three examples of how seemingly adorable clothes that would seem to be the perfect new-baby gift are a nightmare in real life:

- That darling turtleneck-and-overalls outfit that makes the baby mannequin in the store appear to be a mini railroad engineer is actually a torture device for an infant. *You* try pulling a turtleneck over the head of a squirming baby and then changing a diaper under a pair of pants without snaps.

- That dress with the starched collar and stiff lace around the arms may as well be a straitjacket, since that's what it probably feels like to the baby who's wearing it. Also, long dresses are a bear to work with when you're buckling a child into a car seat.

- That gorgeous wool pea coat from the upscale Madison Avenue retailer may as well stay in the box forever. With its "dry clean only" label inside and the spit-up that's sure to land on it sometime during its first wearing, that coat is a goner for sure.

All of this doesn't mean that you shouldn't buy baby clothes as gifts. What you should do is keep the squirmy, fussy, wiggling nature of a baby and the hectic lives of the parents in mind when you shop. Following are my four S's for buying great baby clothes.

Stock Up on Staples

Beyond diapers, there are certain items that new parents can never have enough of. These include one-piece T-shirts that snap in the crotch so they stay tucked in, socks, legging-like pants that slide on and off easily, and hats (babies lose a lot of heat through their heads, so even during the summer, newborns usually have to keep their heads covered). Also, when you buy these, buy them in bulk. That way, the harried parents won't have those extra loads of laundry to do because Sweet Pea has soiled all of his T-shirts.

With shirts, aim for ones that snap down the front or along the shoulders—so the parents don't have to turn slipping a shirt over their baby's head into a flashback of the trip down the birth canal. I know firsthand that a baby is sure to freak out if darkness descends while you pull a shirt over its head. When my daughters were young, I learned to buy (and give as gifts) T-shirts from JC Penney that had an open front that snapped up the middle. There was no trauma involved when putting these on or taking them off.

Think Soft

If there's one thing that's going to make a bambino miserable (besides a dirty diaper, hunger, or sleepiness), it's uncomfortable clothes. Put yourself in the baby's shoes—or pajamas, if you will. I'm definitely a happier person when I'm wearing a soft, comfortable outfit; why should a tyke be any different? When my children were babies, the clothes that we used over and over were those made of soft fabrics, such as terry-cloth footed pajamas and cotton jumpsuits. We also favored stretch fabrics, which came in handy as my kids became more mobile and began creeping along the floor.

❧ The Best Gift I Ever Gave ❧

After we had the twins, I gave my husband a children's book called *Daddy and Me*. It's just pictures of babies and daddies doing different things together—shaving, jumping, tossing a ball, and so forth. Now, every night before they go to bed, he "reads" the twins this book and acts out what he sees in the pictures. It's so cute.

Leslie, New York

Snaps Are a Must

I can't stress enough how important this easy-access thing is, and when it comes to baby clothes, snaps are the way to go. When you have a wailing child and need to get to a dirty diaper quickly, you don't want to fuss with buttons or ties. You want to be able to rip off the soiled clothes and whisk the baby into dry, clean clothes (and thereby put an end to the crying). Trusty snaps pretty much allow you to do that without ruining an outfit. Don't think that zippers will work as well: while they may offer the expediency element, I've known too many parents (myself included) who accidentally zipped their child's tender flesh when getting the baby dressed. So, when in doubt, go with snaps.

Size Up

Until you've had a baby of your own, you have no idea how quickly these little guys can grow. But grow they do. The average baby more than doubles its birth weight by the time it is six months old, and many do so long before the half-year mark. In fact, when they were only two months old, both of my children weighed twice as much as they did when they were born. When you apply that phenomenon to buying clothes for a baby, you realize how ridiculous the newborn size is. Yes, it's usually perfect for a coming-home-from-the-hospital outfit, but a week later, that same outfit will probably be too snug and get handed down as doll clothes. That's why I recommend that people size up (and then some) when shopping for baby clothes.

❧ *The Best Gift I Ever Got* ❦

When I had my first baby, my coworkers sent me several trays of food, loaves of bread, and desserts from an Italian gourmet cafe near my home. I had enough eggplant parmigiana, stuffed manicotti, and baked ziti to eat and freeze for later. All told, that food gave us two weeks' worth of meals, which we really appreciated, since it took me extra long to get up and running after my C-section.

Jennifer, Ohio

Let's say your friend had a bouncing baby boy in August. You just saw the world's cutest cotton sleeper for Christmas and were planning on buying the four-to-six-months size. But don't. While the child will be four months old when Saint Nick pays a visit, there's a good chance that he'll be wearing six-months or bigger clothing. My rule of thumb is this: When in doubt, buy a size bigger. Even when you know the height and weight of the baby and can plot the numbers on a size chart in the store, you should buy the next size up. This guarantees a longer wearing time, since the baby can grow into the outfit, and it covers you if a manufacturer tends to cut clothes on the smaller side, which many do, unfortunately.

Gifts for Religious Ceremonies

Religious ceremonies for newly born children are usually a way of welcoming them into a house of worship and the surrounding community. If you are invited to a bris, a baby naming, or a baptism, it is customary to take a gift, even if you gave or sent something after the child was born. The pressure is compounded if you're one of the godparents.

Gifts for these kinds of ceremonies are usually classified very differently from other "birth" day gifts. In this case, toys are usually a no-no, and anything with a religious connotation is a yes-yes. A fine point to the rule is the silver christening cup, which godparents in the Christian religion tend to give their godchildren at the christening.

Here are some ideas on appropriate gifts to celebrate a newborn's religious service:

- Religious jewelry, such as a small Star of David or a cross—for the Jewish or Christian child, respectively, to wear when older
- An illustrated children's Bible or a Bible storybook
- For Jewish boys, a hand-knit or one-of-a-kind yarmulke (head covering)
- Donation to the child's house of worship or purchase of a dedicated item at that house of worship
- Art, decorative items, or prints of a religious or biblical nature (think anything Noah's Ark)

If you don't have a retail store nearby where you can find these kinds of items, try a museum store, either in person or online. You might also want to check in at a house of worship that has a gift shop affiliated with it. Often, you can find appropriate present ideas there.

❧ The Best Gift I Ever Got ❧

When my daughter was born, one of my mother's friends sent a beautiful pillow made from vintage fabrics and ribbons in pale pink and white. It's monogrammed with my daughter's initials and is truly the centerpiece of her room. I hope she'll pass it on to her children someday.

Kathleen, Pennsylvania

Keep Safety in Mind When Buying Toys

One transformation that usually occurs among parents after the baby is born is that they become the safety police—always on the lookout for dangers to their children. When my first daughter was born, there were news reports that certain kinds of window blinds emitted lead dust, and others posed a choking hazard. When we checked our windows, we discovered that we owned both of these kinds of blinds and promptly took them down.

What, you may be asking, do window blinds have to do with buying a baby gift? The answer is that they illustrate how something so seemingly innocuous could harm a child, and you wouldn't even know it. In my case, it was the blinds, something I'd purchased to decorate my home. For you, it could be that irresistible stuffed animal that you saw at the store, or a toy with small pieces that a baby could choke on. Stuffed animals and toys that have small pieces should be shunned from your list of possible baby gifts; they are better suited for older children.

The same goes for toys with long strings attached; the strings can wrap around a baby's neck.

For a heads-up about safe toys, including alerts to recalled toys, check out the website of the Consumer Products Safety Commission at cpsc.gov.

Don't Forget the Big Brother or Big Sister

When a baby is born, people sometimes forget that the child who was there before is also excited about having a new sibling and deserves a present to celebrate his or her new role in life as big brother or big sister. You don't need to go all out on a present for the older child; just make sure you get something. When you arrive to wish the new baby well, have a little wrapped present for any other children in the family to open and enjoy so they don't feel left out from all the excitement. Some fun gifts that my daughter Jane received when her sister Anne arrived were a pint-size apron and cooking utensils (so she could help Mommy and Daddy in the kitchen), and crayons and coloring books. They weren't big, but they meant a lot to her—and to us, too.

Baby Showers

Chances are if you know someone who is pregnant, you're going to be invited to a baby shower. These traditionally women-only gatherings usually feature a variety of silly games (such as identifying the baby food in an unlabeled jar) that would carry any modern woman back to her domestic roots. I've given and attended countless baby showers, and they are worlds apart from bridal showers.

A "Babyography"

Want to present a unique gift to a baby—a gift that is as one-of-a-kind as the child? Then, I direct you to the "Babyography" offered by the All About Baby company in Thousand Oaks, California. This eleven-by-fourteen-inch certificate provides a capsule of the day the child was born: in addition to the basic birth-certificate information, a "Babyography" includes fun facts about the child's birthday as well as trends during the year. Best of all, the certificate has whimsical illustrations such as alphabet blocks, a teddy bear, and a doll. It's perfect for framing and hanging in the nursery. For more information contact All About Baby at (805) 373-5197 or online at allbaby.com.

At a bridal shower, it's often the first time that both sides of the betrothed couple's family are socializing, which can make for some really awkward moments. By the time a baby shower rolls around, on the other hand, the principals have survived a wedding and probably a couple of holidays together, and everyone is more relaxed. And as far as baby shower gifts go, I say anything goes for the mother, the bundle of joy, and, if you want to cover all your bases, the father, too.

If you're lucky, the mother-to-be has registered (yes, you can do that now for events beyond weddings). If so, get thee a copy of her registry list, and go shopping for some of her must-have items. If you want to get a big-ticket purchase, suggest a few people chip in together. Obvious must-haves include car seats, strollers, baby carriers, and changing tables.

Even without a registry list to direct you, you can confidently pick out a great gift if you know the basics. One of the best gifts I ever received was a large Rubbermaid storage bin filled with diapers in a range of sizes, baby wipes, and diaper-rash cream. It probably didn't cost much money, but it was extremely thoughtful and practical. I put the contents to use the very day we came home from the hospital. And the bin came in handy for keeping baby clothes that my daughter outgrew and that I knew I'd eventually use with another child, which I did. Now, years later that bin sits in my basement, storing off-season clothes. Talk about the gift that keeps on giving.

Other no-fail gifts include:

- *Baby clothes.* Just remember the four S's mentioned earlier.

- *Children's books.* Buying books that your own children enjoyed will make the gift more meaningful—especially if you tell the parents this in an inscription.

- *Bibs.* These are always helpful, and spitters—babies who spit up a lot—go through multiple bibs per day, so this gift is bound to get a workout. Bibs are also extremely useful once the baby starts eating solid food and feeding becomes a one step forward, two steps back event, with most of the food ending up outside the baby's mouth.

- *Spill-proof "sippy" cups.* Many babies make the transition right from the breast or bottle to a sippy cup, so this will be a much-needed item a few months down the road.

- *CDs.* My cousin presented my husband and me with a Raffi CD after my first daughter was born, and a friend gave us a Peter, Paul, and Mary CD with "Puff, the Magic Dragon" on it. (That was one of my favorite songs as a child.) Those two recordings became the soundtrack of our life during those first few months as parents, and I'm sure other new parents or soon-to-be new parents would appreciate these kind of CDs as gifts as well.

- *Picture frames and photo albums.* New parents take lots and lots of pictures of their bundle of joy. They'll definitely want to show off the photos of their adorable baby, and a picture frame or photo album lets them do it in style. Parents looking to splurge on a new-parent gift for their son or daughter, the new parent, may want to give a camera (video or still) as well.

- *Something for the expectant mother.* I know a woman who received a gift certificate to a spa for a pregnancy massage, followed by a manicure and pedicure, courtesy of her office colleagues. They told her that they assumed the remaining months of her pregnancy would be the last time she'd be able to indulge herself, so they wanted to help her do that. What fabulous, thoughtful friends this woman has, and if you're looking for a present just for the mother-to-be, this is a great idea.

Whatever you select to celebrate the new arrival, include a gift receipt for any purchase. That way, if for any reason the parents need to return the item, they'll know where you bought it (but not how much you spent), and you'll have made making the refund or exchange much easier for them.

❧ 3 ❧

ALL ABOUT ANNIVERSARIES

I mentioned in the introduction that each year, Americans give, on average, about 50 gifts a year. I imagine that one occasion for which they're buying gifts regularly is someone's anniversary—whether it's their parents, their siblings or even their own spouse. What's great about an anniversary gift is that it changes every year, thanks to the predetermined gift themes, which I'll talk about in a little bit. However, for most people unless someone is celebrating a milestone anniversary where gift selections are obvious—such as for a couple that's been married twenty-five years and is celebrating its silver anniversary, where an appropriate gift would be something silver—most people are stumped. For example, my husband and I are coming up on our thirteenth wedding anniversary, and even I have to wonder: what does one buy to commemorate a thirteenth anniversary? Perhaps you're rusty on these gift-giving traditions, too.

Gift Giving FYI

A great resource for gifts containing some of the more unusual anniversary themes, such as willow and textiles, is the Berea College Crafts catalog and website (berea.com). The Kentucky college's crafts program, staffed with students and faculty, helps support the tuition-free status of this liberal arts school in the Appalachian region. The catalog and website are bursting with high-quality handmade crafts, including willow walking sticks ($15) and hand-woven table runners ($25) and place-mats ($9 each), along with wood crafts, hand-blown glass objets d'art, and pottery.

Anniversary Gift Themes

I'm happy to report that you no longer have to be stymied—nor do I. In researching this chapter, I was able to pull together a comprehensive list of anniversary gift themes—both the classic and modern versions. On the next few pages, I'll tell you what these themes are, and then I'll offer appropriate gift suggestions. Now, while lesser shoppers may remain baffled about what to give for someone's thirteenth anniversary, as I was earlier this year, if you read on, you'll learn that looking to a gift of lace, textiles or fur would be right on target.

A good catchall gift for any of the anniversary themes is a book that is related to the theme. Need a fourth-anniversary gift that involves flowers? Perhaps the couple would like to pore through a coffee-table book on annuals and perennials. For an eleventh-anniversary gift featuring steel, it won't be hard to produce a book about cars, a biography of Henry Ford, or, for the comic book lover, a compilation about the Man of Steel—Superman.

Before I get into specific suggestions, I should point out that there are certain five-year stretches of married life for which, as far as I can tell, no one has ever designated an appropriate gift theme. For example, you'll notice that my list skips from the fifteenth anniversary right to the twentieth. So, what do you do for anniversaries sixteen through nineteen? One option is to apply any of the general gift-giving advice packed in this book, such as the all-occasion appropriateness of housewares or gifts that reflect hobbies (especially ones the couple enjoys together).

In addition, for some reason, certain items appear as a theme more than once, such as wood, which is considered a classic gift for a fifth anniversary but a modern gift for a sixth anniversary. Similarly, leather is a classic gift for a third anniversary but a modern gift for the ninth. Rather than repeat myself throughout the chapter, I offer detailed gift ideas the first time a particular theme appears. Then later, when it appears again, I refer you back to my initial suggestions. In addition, I hope that the more you see my suggested idea, the more you'll begin to brainstorm gift ideas on your own. When in doubt you can always plug in one of the anniversary gift themes into a search engine like Google or an online auction portal like eBay and see what comes up. You may be surprised to find excellent gift ideas right on your computer.

One timely tip on buying anniversary gifts for others is this: plan ahead, starting when they first get married. That is, when you're shopping for a wedding gift using a couple's registry list as your guide, don't throw that list away once you've made your purchase. It will come in handy years from now when you're searching for an appropriate anniversary gift. Since most retailers keep a registry list active only until a couple's first anniversary (some not even that long), you won't have access to it when you're searching for a fifth-anniversary gift. That's why it pays to plan ahead and keep that list on file.

First Anniversary
CLASSIC: *Paper*   MODERN: *Clocks*

Even though clocks are designated the modern first-anniversary gift, I think there's nothing more classic than a fine-quality timepiece. A husband could choose a watch with a fancy face for his wife, and the wife could give her husband a similarly nice watch or a decorative clock for his desk at work.

With the classic gift of paper, you have a full measure of options. You can stick to the straight and narrow and give a book or a gift certificate to a bookstore. Or you can order personalized stationery. A wife could give her husband notepaper with his monogram, or vice versa. More creative types can assemble a unique scrapbook of the couple's life together so far: this can include pictures from their dating days, or even earlier, notes of funny things they said as they were planning their wedding, souvenirs from the ceremony and reception, such as match-book covers or a copy of the invitation, and photographs from the honeymoon. Going in another direction, tickets to a concert also qualify as a gift of paper. Don't be afraid to have a little fun as you consider all the paper-related possibilities for this first anniversary gift.

Second Anniversary
CLASSIC: *Cotton*   MODERN: *China*

The first thing that comes to mind when I think of cotton is something soft and wearable. Cotton flannel pajamas may warm the heart of that special someone to whom you've been married for two years; or, for a couple, you could try to find matching sets of pajamas. (I know country's all-star couple Faith Hill and Tim McGraw recently gave each other matching cotton flannel pajamas, so you'd be in good company.) You could also extend the sleep theme to include two-hundred-plus-thread-count cotton pillowcases or a pretty cotton quilt.

Daytime clothing also fits the category. I would have been glad to receive a cotton twin sweater set for my second anniversary, and I'm sure my husband would have dug a cotton T-shirt from his alma mater.

If instead you go for the modern version of the second-anniversary gift, you can fill in the gaps in a couple's china pattern with a soup tureen or serving platter—one example of why keeping someone's registry on hand can pay off. Or, if you and your spouse never completed your china, you can buy each other a place setting—or suggest that family and friends do something similar when they ask what you'd like for your anniversary. Another idea might be to treat them to dinner at a Chinese restaurant or one with "China" in the name. Feeling especially adventurous? Why not book a trip to the real China as part of your anniversary celebration.

Third Anniversary
CLASSIC: *Leather*   MODERN: *Crystal or Glass*

I don't know about you, but I can never have enough crystal or cut glass to decorate my home. I like to use these beautiful pieces to hold flowers or to use for serving food when company comes over. Because of the nature of this modern third-anniversary gift, I think it's perfectly appropriate to go a little on the expensive side and seek out a crystal gift from a top-quality manufacturer like Waterford, Steuben, or Tiffany. Or, as with the second anniversary, you can refer to the recipient's gift registry list for a preference in stemware, which easily qualify in the crystal category. Since pieces inevitably break or chip through wear and tear, supplying someone with an additional four crystal stems as an anniversary gift makes elegant sense.

With the gift of leather, it is important that you stick with classy and conservative gift ideas—avoid gag items or anything overtly sexual. In other words, stay away from chaps and leather teddies, even though it might seem funny to you. It could embarrass the gift recipient. Instead, you should focus on presents from high-end stores that specializes in leather goods, such as Coach or Louis Vuitton—a world-class luggage and handbag maker. You usually can't go wrong with a leather belt, wallet, or business card holder. I've also seen lovely leather photo albums and frames at these kinds of stores.

Fourth Anniversary
CLASSIC: *Fruit or Flowers*   MODERN: *Electrical Appliances*

If you opt for the classic fourth-anniversary gift of fruit or flowers, you can get off pretty easy—whether it be for your spouse or someone else. Just send flowers or a gift basket of fruit, and you're done. If you go this route, choose a reputable vendor—one you've used previously and with whom you had a good experience, or a national company known for excellence. Two such companies that offer top-notch fruit and flowers are 1-800-FLOWERS and Harry and David.

As to the notion of a modern anniversary gift of electrical appliances, you can think big or you can think small. I mean, both a label maker and a refrigerator could be an appropriate electrical appliance for a fourth-anniversary gift, but they may seem a bit odd. A better bet is to buy an appliance that you know your spouse or the couple you're targeting has been eyeing, such as a high-end coffeemaker or a cooking tool from the Food Network. If you're in the dark, you can always fall back on a gift certificate from a store that carries electrical appliances, such as Staples or Lowe's, or a retailer of digital technology tools such as Radio Shack or Best Buy.

Fifth Anniversary
CLASSIC: *Wood*   MODERN: *Silverware*

When you think of a quintessential wood-themed gift, what do you think? If I'm going for a present that represents the viability of a couple's marriage, I would think about giving them the gift of a tree that they could use to decorate their yard or a potted tree for inside the house. A couple celebrating their fifth anniversary during warm-weather months can plan to spend a day picking out a fruit-bearing or flowering tree at a local nursery and then planting it in their yard. Another avenue is to make the gift philanthropic: if the couple is of Jewish descent, have a tree planted in Israel in their name; or make a donation on the couple's behalf to the National Arbor Day Foundation, which is responsible for planting nearly 450,000 trees across America and offers a Rain Forest Rescue program to help save trees abroad.

For a gift that doesn't need to be watered, you can limit yourself to something made from wood—a humidor for the guy who likes cigars, or a mahogany jewelry box for the gal who never knows where to put her earrings and necklaces. Wooden birdhouses or picture frames are also low maintenance. And if you want to spring for something big, you can move up to a piece of wooden furniture.

The modern version of the fifth-anniversary gift—silverware—is pretty straightforward: all you've got to think about is buying forks, knives, and spoons. Ideally, they should match the couple's existing set. If it's a gift for each other, maybe you use this anniversary as an excuse to replace your mismatched silverware with a design you've always admired.

Sixth Anniversary
CLASSIC: *Candy or Iron*   MODERN: *Wood*

For creative gift ideas of items made from iron, I would suggest looking in your yellow pages for a local ironsmith whose shop you could visit. If there isn't a store near you, keep your eye out for craft fairs, where there's usually at least one ironsmith selling custom wares. In this category, I have a fondness for hanging pot racks, iron doorstops, and andirons for the fireplace. I've also seen fabulous iron products sold through shop-at-home companies like Southern Living at Home or kitchen-centric companies like Le Creuset, so you shouldn't have any trouble finding something made from iron.

The other classic sixth-anniversary gift is a hands-down favorite: candy. It's hard to find fault with a delicious box of sweets to celebrate being married six years. It's like Halloween, only better. Either a husband or wife could put together a big gift basket of the spouse's favorite treats and present that as the, well, present.

Here's a more adventurous option: Go on a weekend trip with your spouse to a nearby town where candy is made, and take a behind-the-scenes tour of the factory. You're guaranteed to get to sample lots of goodies. Best of all, most company factory tours are free. Here are two candy tours to consider:

Hershey Chocolate

In Hershey, Pennsylvania, the streets are practically paved with chocolate, since Hershey Foods is the dominating presence in this eponymous town near Harrisburg. You'll love the street lamps shaped like Hershey's Kisses, and if you're a chocoholic like I am, you'll really love the simulated chocolate-making tour at the Hershey's Chocolate World Visitor's Center. At the end, you get free samples. Check out the "Discovery Hershey" link on the Hershey website at hersheys.com for more information.

For West Coasters, a Hershey factory tour is also available in the Golden State. It's at the company plant in Oakdale, California, where Hershey's Kisses are made. You'll want to click on the "Hershey's Oakdale" link on the same website, once you click through to "Discover Hershey," for more information on arranging a visit. There's also a visitors center and factory tour available in Ontario, at Smith Falls, which is between Toronto and Montreal. (FYI, there are Hershey stores to satisfy your sweet tooth in New York City's Times Square and Chicago, too.)

Jelly Belly Jelly Beans

The Herman Goelitz Company makes Jelly Belly jelly beans and Gummi candies in its Fairfield, California, plant outside Oakland. Visitors are welcome to tour the facility and taste freshly made jelly beans seven days a week. If you don't get enough to eat on the tour, the gift shop sells hundreds of varieties of yummy Gummies and delicious Jelly Belly products, including two-pound bags of rejected (yet still good to eat) jelly beans called "Belly Flops." There's a similar factory and tour at the company's location on the border of Illinois and Wisconsin, on the Milwaukee-Chicago corridor of Interstate 94. You can get more information on either tour location at the company's website jellybelly.com—just click on the "Find a Store" link.

❧ *The Best Gift I Ever Got* ❧

Now that we have kids, my husband and I have decided that it's silly to spend lots of money on anniversary gifts for each other. So, on our last anniversary, we got a sitter and just went out to dinner. After the meal, my husband started pulling out all these wrapped gifts, one after another. He'd broken our rule, and I felt bad that I didn't have anything for him. But then I started unwrapping the gifts, and inside each box was some of my favorite candy. One box had chocolates, another had candy corn, and then another had a large Peppermint Patty. It was a lot of fun to open the gifts and then eat them later. At least he hadn't spent a lot of money, as we'd originally agreed.

Leslie, New York

For more great ideas on candy factories to tour for your sixth anniversary, look in a copy of *Watch It Made in the U.S.A.* by Karen Axelrod and Bruce Brumberg, which describes nearly three hundred factory tours open to the public, from candy makers to car manufacturers. (You can get more information about the book and factory tours in general at the authors' website factorytour.com.)

For ideas on a modern sixth-anniversary gift made from wood, you can turn back a couple of pages and revisit the gift suggestions I made for the fifth anniversary, when wood is considered to be a "classic" anniversary gift.

Seventh Anniversary
CLASSIC: *Wool or Copper*   MODERN: *Desk Sets*

I have a relative who is a proficient knitter, and I'm always thrilled when she gives me a handmade wool sweater or throw. If you have a similar knack, and you need a seventh-anniversary gift to give to someone, why not grab a ball of wool and knit one, purl two? Not only would it be appropriate for the anniversary, but it would also carry lasting sentiment, since you made it yourself. Of course, the same applies if you should happen to be a coppersmith. Make your favorite couple a stunning sculpture out of copper, and you'll be revered forever in their hearts.

Now, let's say you're restricted to more traditional means for producing a seventh-anniversary gift—say, the mall. No problem. Search out a pair of matching wool sweaters or a wool blanket. If you prefer to look for gifts made of copper, you can search your favorite cooking store (brick and mortar, or online) for functional but sleek pots or other cooking utensils.

For the modern version of the seventh-anniversary gift, the desk set, I suggest a high-end pen set or coordinated desk accessories. In the latter case, you should know the decorating style of the office of the person or persons receiving the gift. You wouldn't want to present an op art desk set to someone whose office is done in a Shaker style.

Eighth Anniversary

CLASSIC: *Bronze or Pottery* MODERN: *Linens or Lace*

With four themes to choose from, coming up with an eighth-anniversary gift should be a cinch. Since both bronze and pottery have artistic implications, you and your spouse could consider giving each other the gift of a class or workshop on bronze sculpture or pottery through a local studio or community college. Or, if your schedules preclude that kind of time commitment, celebrate your anniversary by going out to dinner and then to a paint-your-own-pottery place, where you can spend the evening making each other a gift. This idea is also a great idea for children looking to give their parents an eighth-anniversary gift.

A luxurious gift from a husband to a wife involving linens and lace, the modern anniversary gift theme, is a set of high-thread-count sheets (they're the softest) and some lace lingerie to go along with it. If you're buying for a couple, table linens and lace table accessories would do nicely, as would a gift certificate from a store where they can choose for themselves,. One such appropriately named retailer would be Linens 'n Things.

Ninth Anniversary

CLASSIC: *Pottery or Willow* MODERN: *Leather*

We've covered pottery (eighth) and leather (third), so you should already have some ideas to toss around for a ninth anniversary gift. That leaves us with willow. And I wonder if you had the same reaction that I did when I first discovered the concept of a willow gift: What the heck is that? Fear not, dear reader, I have an answer and a solution.

The willow gift, simply, must have something to do with a willow tree. There are all kinds of willows—weeping willows, corkscrew willows, and pussy willows (more a reed than a tree). That means that your willow-related gift options could include planting a willow tree in your yard in honor of your ninth anniversary or buying the happily married couple a piece of furniture or other decorative item made of a willow's trademark bent wood, such as a door wreath. If you'd like to go for an utterly simple yet romantic gift, you could present your beloved with a bouquet of pussy willows tied with a pretty ribbon.

Tenth Anniversary

CLASSIC: *Tin or Aluminum*   MODERN: *Diamond Jewelry*

For movie buffs that have been married for ten years and are celebrating their anniversary, videos of films with the word *tin* in the title would be a cool gift to give. These include *Pushing Tin, Tin Cup, Cat on a Hot Tin Roof,* and *Tin Men.* For collectors, you could search eBay or a local antiques fair for old-fashioned tin toys or tin lunchboxes.

Moving on to aluminum, instead of giving a gift of aluminum, how about using aluminum foil as your gift wrap? For example, a husband could buy his wife a modern tenth-anniversary gift—diamond jewelry—and wrap the box in aluminum foil as a way of touching on the classic gift theme as well. If you're feeling a little zany and you're adept at folding aluminum foil into shapes, make the package look like a swan or some other figure, the way some restaurants do with doggy bags. Your beloved may be momentarily confused when presented with a gift that looks like leftover food, but that confusion will turn to delight when it reveals the diamond jewelry inside.

Eleventh Anniversary

CLASSIC: *Steel*   MODERN: *Jewelry*

When you think of steel, do you think of a cold, hard metal? Believe it or not, this metal can be the inspiration for warm and loving eleventh-anniversary gifts. Just consider the possibilities:

- Treat a football fan to a Pittsburgh Steelers game—whether they're the hometown team or the opponents.
- Hire a steel drum band to serenade a loved one with "your" song, such as the song you danced to during your wedding's first dance. You could take this notion one step further and steal away to a Caribbean country

for your anniversary, where you could listen to a homegrown and live steel drum band during your trip.

- Buy a set of high-end stainless steel cutlery or cookware.
- Present the handyman husband with a new set of tools made from steel.
- Get your spouse a new car.

With the generic jewelry theme of an eleventh-anniversary gift, your options are limitless—and admittedly skewed more to the wife than the husband. For a woman, you can't lose with earrings, a necklace, a bracelet, or a ring. For a man, you can present him with cuff links, a simple chain, or a new ring to match the wife's. If you've enjoyed traveling together, try to find a piece of jewelry, such as a pin, that represents where you've been.

Twelfth Anniversary
CLASSIC: *Silk or Linens*   MODERN: *Pearls*

While linen-related gifts should be fresh in your mind from the eighth-anniversary section, we've yet to touch on the subject of silk, a most glorious fabric. There are a number of wonderful silk gifts you and your spouse can get for each other or that you can give to a couple you know.

I think a marvelous gift that a husband can give to his wife and vice versa is silk underwear. Most guys really like how it feels to wear silk boxer shorts but probably can't justify buying a pair for themselves. Likewise, most women are drawn to the elegance of silk lingerie but see it as an indulgence. What better gift could there be to give than something like silk underwear, which you know the other person will enjoy but would never buy on his or her own? I say go for it.

When you want to find a gift something less intimate than silk lingerie, you have a rainbow of choices with silk ties for him and silk scarves for her. Better yet, if business travel takes you to Asia, buy your silk gifts there. This region is known for its silk production, and your gift will mean all the more because it came from the other side of the world.

If you prefer pearls, the modern twelfth-anniversary gift, you can always buy her pearl jewelry. For him, look for items made with mother-of-pearl, such as a pocketknife, a watch fob, or cuff links.

Thirteenth Anniversary
CLASSIC: *Lace* MODERN: *Textiles or Fur*

If you're not sure what qualifies as a textile gift, consider this: Webster's defines *textile* as cloth, especially woven or knit cloth. You could extrapolate this theme in a variety of ways: a hand-painted cloth tapestry for the home, an article of clothing, or a handmade quilt. You could even extend the meaning to include long-term benefits: stock in a textile company.

The other modern gift does have its pros and cons. Today's society doesn't look as kindly on fur as a fashion statement as it once did, so if you're not sure how the recipient will react to such a gift, escape the controversy with either the textile or lace theme. (For lace, turn back to the section on eighth anniversary gifts for some of my suggestions.) However, if you're buying something for a woman who has been gushing that she'd love to own a fur coat or just a stole, then this anniversary would qualify as the time to fulfill that wish.

Coming down a step, you could always give fur with a collar—and a leash. If your family has been talking about getting a pet, use your thirteenth anniversary as your reason to finally adopt that dog, cat, hamster, or guinea pig to the household. Another option is to explore many types of fur beyond the kind that you wear or would keep as a pet in your home. For example, you could spend your anniversary at a place filled with furry friends—at the zoo.

Fourteenth Anniversary
CLASSIC: *Ivory* MODERN: *Gold Jewelry*

Because acquiring raw ivory usually involves killing certain animals, I think it's best to eschew items actually made from ivory when considering your gift options. Many countries have banned them. That said, there's nothing wrong with giving a gift the color of ivory—such as a china vase. Or play on the theme with a gift related to pianos. "Tickling the ivories" can take the form of tickets to a piano concert or a CD of a famous pianist. Prime choices might be well-known contemporary pianists like Alicia Keys, Billy Joel, Elton John, or classical composer Debussy.

With gold jewelry, maybe this is the anniversary when you buy each other new gold wedding bands. Earrings, a bracelet, or a necklace made from gold would also make the grade.

Fifteenth Anniversary
CLASSIC: *Crystal*   MODERN: *Watch*

As with the first and third anniversaries, in regard to gifts involving clocks and crystal, respectively, you can't go wrong with nice watches for you and your spouse or a decorative piece of cut crystal from a high-end company such as Tiffany or Waterford. A twist on the watch gift could be something involving Salvador Dali's well-known dripping watches: tickets to see a museum exhibit of his work, or a print or set of notepaper featuring this surreal image. For additional ideas on gifts in these themes, turn back to the sections on first and third anniversaries.

Twentieth Anniversary
CLASSIC: *China*   MODERN: *Platinum*

When the originators of anniversary gift themes chose china, I'm sure they were thinking of the kind you register for when you're getting married. But if you were to do a variation on a theme, wouldn't it be wonderful to celebrate your anniversary by taking a trip to China? As with travel to any foreign country, going to China requires some preparation, especially since the Chinese government views personal rights differently from the way the American government does. Nonetheless, thousands of people travel to China regularly for business and pleasure and sing its praises. So, if it's an option, don't pass up the opportunity to create a memorable vacation and anniversary celebration.

If world-traveling isn't your cup of tea, choose the more sedate gift of something made of china. Or go with the modern version of the twentieth-anniversary gift, something made from platinum.

Platinum is considered to be one of the world's most resilient metals because it retains its sheen over time, and it complements precious gems in a way no other metal does. It's also very expensive, which is another reason it's so desirable. Any type of platinum gift would be overwhelmingly appreciated.

Post-Twentieth Anniversary

As luck would have it, there are no anniversary gift guidelines for twenty-first through twenty-fourth anniversaries. They begin again at the twenty-fifth anniversary, also known as a silver anniversary. That means that when choosing gifts for one of these anniversaries without a theme, the sky's the limit. Just don't wimp out and buy nothing. Even if you only remember to send a card, at least you will have celebrated the person's anniversary, albeit in small way.

Silver Anniversary and Beyond

From this anniversary on, all of the themes, which occur in five-year increments, revolve around precious metals or gemstones. That makes jewelry the most obvious gift between husbands and wives—perhaps earrings or a pin for her, cuff links or a ring for him. Furthermore, as you get up in years of marriage, classic and modern versions of designated anniversary gifts finally come together. So, if you're lucky enough to be married for a quarter century or more—or if a couple close to you is—anniversary gift giving will get easier. Here are the classic and modern themes for you to consider buying as a gift to help mark the occasion:

Anniversary	*Classic*	*Modern*
Twenty-Fifth	Silver	Silver
Thirtieth	Pearls	Diamond Jewelry
Thirty-Fifth	Coral	Jade
Fortieth	Ruby	Ruby
Forty-Fifth	Sapphire	Sapphire
Fiftieth	Gold	Gold
Fifty-Fifth	Emerald	Emerald
Sixtieth	Diamond	Diamond
Seventy-Fifth	Diamond (again)	Diamond (again)

❧ 4 ❧

BEST BETS FOR BIRTHDAYS

If our family's gift-giving decisions were left to my daughters, everyone would receive a doll for birthdays, Christmas, Chanukah, and all other gift-giving occasions. To them, the choice is as plain as the nose on their face: because *they* enjoy playing with dolls more than anything else in the whole world, they naively reason that everyone else would love to receive one. And when we need to buy a birthday gift for one of their school friends, you can usually find us shopping in one of those very pink shopping aisles at the local toy store. While my daughters would love to own every (expensive) American Girl doll, when it comes to shopping for them and their friends' birthdays, we generally confine our purchases to a couple of the more affordable dolls and maybe some accessories to go with them. I bet most other parents are like me: we want our children to be able to play with a birthday gift with reckless abandon—and not have to worry that when Ken's head falls off, we've just tossed a ton of money down the toilet.

Quick Tips

To personalize your gift wrapping, invest in plain brown paper and a playful assortment of rubber stamps and ink pads. Then decorate the paper with images that relate to the gift-giving occasion or to the recipient's likes in general. For example, for a child who's intrigued by trains, planes, and automobiles, you can decorate with images of these modes of transportation. You can also adapt this type of decoration for other occasions, including Valentine's Day (hearts and flowers), Christmas and Chanukah (images of the season), and baby showers (anything in the nursery—booties, bottles, rattles).

❧ The Best Gift I Ever Gave ❧

Two years ago, I took time off to fly to Calgary to be with my brother on his fiftieth birthday. He didn't know I was coming. He answered the front door and burst into tears when he saw me standing there. I had a four-day visit, during which we skied, sang, and raised a glass (or two) to his fiftieth. The real gift, I believe, was the gift of time and my being able to be there to celebrate with him. I'm really close to my brother, but because we live so far apart, we don't get to see each other as much as we'd like. Since that first gift of time, my husband has done the same for his parents' birthdays, and recently we pooled our frequent-flier miles so that my husband's youngest sister could visit her parents and siblings on the West Coast for her fortieth birthday. What we've learned is that perhaps the most important gift on Earth is time spent with those we love.

Katharine, Quebec

❧ The Best Gift I Ever Got ❧

I'm a real outdoorsy type of person, so I was thrilled when I got an Appalachian Mountain Club membership as a birthday gift one year. What was cool was that my gift came packaged in a sports bottle along with the AMC magazine, *Outdoors,* and discount coupons to use on lodging and training. I've continued to renew my membership, and I go out and hike the White Mountains whenever I can.

Jim, Massachusetts

Finding the Perfect Birthday Gift

You wouldn't buy a grown-up a doll as a birthday gift—unless this adult happens to be a doll collector—but you can learn an important gift-giving lesson from my children: When you're not sure what to buy someone for a birthday, choose something that you enjoy yourself and which you're reasonably certain the gift recipient will enjoy as well.

I don't mean to suggest that you give a meat-of-the-month-club membership to your sister who is an avowed vegetarian, but if you're at a loss for a gift, think back to some of the things you've enjoyed—and that would likely please the recipient in the same way. For example (and I know this sounds cliché), have you read any good books lately? Heard an awesome CD? Sipped a wine that was just superb? These are the kinds of questions you need to ask yourself as you contemplate prospective gifts.

In addition, as I mentioned earlier in the book, knowing the recipient's hobbies or pastimes can help clue you in on the optimum gift choice.

For example, my mother is a bird-watching fan like no other I've ever met. She keeps a pair of binoculars and a guide to North American birds on her kitchen table (and did when I was growing up) so that whenever she spots an interesting feathered friend in the trees, she can watch it with her binoculars, and then look it up in her book. Naturally enough, I often buy her bird-related gifts for her birthday. One year, we bought her some beautiful bird notepaper from the Metropolitan Museum of Art store. Another year, we had some fun and got a T-shirt from the Signals catalog illustrated with the bird poop markings of various species. Not long ago, at my local Lenox store, I spied a set of cake plates with a North American birds motif, and they are at the top of this year's idea list for Mom.

A challenge in giving birthday gifts to people you've known for a long time is whether or not your gifts should change over time. It should for sure when you're giving gifts to younger folks. While your nephew might have loved his annual Play-Doh loot for birthdays throughout elementary school, he'll probably think you are weird and outdated if you continue this tradition into his double-digit years. That's why this chapter neatly lays out birthday gift ideas for children, teenagers (for me, the most fickle and difficult group to buy for), and grown-ups—including grandparents. You'll even solve the riddle of what to give your childhood friends' children whom you do not know well.

❧ *The Best Gift I Ever Gave* ❧

One year, I was stumped as to what to give my husband for his birthday, and I recalled how much he'd talked about a trip he'd taken to Cameroon years ago. It just so happened that a Museum of African Art had recently opened in our town, so I bought him a membership. Over the years, I've renewed the membership, and we've enjoyed going for members-only events. Just yesterday, he commented to me how much he appreciates the museum and how membership was a perfect gift for him.

Carol, New York

> ### ❧ *The Best Gift I Ever Gave* ❧
>
> For my mother's sixtieth birthday, my sister and I put together a memo-
> ry book of my mother's life. We sent out a page to friends, family mem-
> bers, coworkers, and the like, and asked them to write something special
> that they remembered about my mother. We also requested that they
> attach a picture of themselves, ideally one with my mother in it. People
> offered great things—some poems, some just photos. It not only gave
> my sister and me additional insight into our mother's life, but it also
> reminded us how many people she'd touched. My mother was equally
> touched when she received it. Now that memory book has a special place
> in my life, since my mother died a few years ago, and it's a great way for
> me to remember her and what a great lady she was.
>
> *Jeanne, New York*

Quick Tips

Does your gift recipient have a favorite local store—especially an eatery or a food shop?
If so, why not buy him or her a gift package or certificate from that business? For example, we have a close friend who loves our small town's French bakery, whose owners
moved from Paris and brought with them all of their pastry-making know-how. For his
birthday last year, we bought him a gift certificate from this bakery so he could indulge
in croissants and cakes to his heart's delight. Someone else 1 know sent a New Yorker-
cum-Los Angelino a box of bagels from the transplant's beloved Manhattan bagel shop as
a birthday gift one year. The gift was devoured in a New York minute.

Gifts for Children

Before I get into specific gift suggestions, let's all fess up to something: It's just so
easy to buy kids clothes as a birthday gift—especially infants, toddlers, and young
children. You step into baby Gap or Gymboree, and the outfit selections are so
fetching that you want to buy out the store. I know. I've been there and done
that, and I've learned that, while giving a cute outfit can work as *part* of a gift for
a preschool or school-aged child, it shouldn't be all that you give. Here's why: The
next time you're invited to a children's birthday party, watch the collective reac-

tion when the child opens a gift with clothes in it. The adults will probably ooh and aah, accompanied by a group-wide groan from the children. To a kid, there is nothing fun about getting clothing as a gift. To a kid, toys rule, and that's why toys should always be your first gift choice when shopping for kids.

Gift Giving FYI

How old is the birthday party? The Lenox Gift Company, maker of china and porcelain collectibles, did some checking. Here's a look at its collection of birthday facts:

- The first birthday celebration on record happened around 3000 B.C. Only high-ranking officials, such as Egyptian pharaohs, kings, queens, and noblemen, celebrated their birthdays.

- With the rise of Christianity, birthday celebrations ceased. However, once the world starting celebrating Christmas (the birth of Christ) in the fourth century, birthday celebrations for everyone began anew.

- The birthday party that we know of today actually began in thirteenth-century Germany and was called "Kinderfeste," or a celebration for young children. It involved a birthday cake with candles that stayed lit all day, gifts for the birthday boy or girl, and serving that child's favorite meal.

❧ *The Best Gift I Ever Got* ❧

For my fiftieth birthday, my wife sent me to the Richard Petty Driving Experience. I'm a real NASCAR fanatic, as is my wife, so this was a really cool gift. Here's how it works: I got about one hour of instruction, and then I got to drive an actual Winston Cup car around the track at Richmond (Va.) International Raceway for eight laps. My fastest lap was 106 mph. For a race fan, driving a real race car on a real NASCAR track is a dream come true!

Hank, Virginia

There is a notable exception to this rule, though: dress-up clothes do not count as regular clothing and can be purchased without reservation for any child who shows an affinity for this kind of pretend play. Likewise, an athletic uniform or shirt emblazoned with the number of the child's favorite sport star will most likely count as cool clothing.

So, what toys are good for kids? Here are some general rules to keep in mind as you begin your shopping:

- With babies, give a child-safe toy (read the label or box for indications on age appropriateness) that the infant can grip and that makes noise. A wiggle worm with a rattle in its tail was one of my children's early favorites.

- Toddlers and preschoolers love to use their bodies, so anything that gives them freedom to run, push, or build something is key. Stacking cups, a pretend lawn mower, or a child-size baby carriage for taking their dolls on a walk will be used and loved.

- Children of elementary school age have more sophisticated taste in toys and tend to favor games, either board or electronic. One that I fondly remember and that is was among my daughter's top picks when she was in kindergarten was Chutes and Ladders, an exceptionally simple board game. Another perennial pick is Candy Land. Now that my children are older, they favor older board games, such as Clue, Risk and Life. If you're unsure what a ten-year-old would like to receive, ask one. When you're roaming through a store such as Target or Toys R Us looking for a present, stop parents with a child in tow who looks about the age of your gift recipient and ask what that child likes to play with. This informal polling of your target audience should point you in the right direction.

❧ The Best Gift I Ever Gave ❧

I have an eighty-nine-year-old widowed mother who still lives alone, is reasonably active, doesn't drive, and has everything she needs. She tells us each year that she wants nothing for her birthday. Last year, we came up with a creative solution. My siblings and I, along with our fourteen grown children and their sixteen children, sent her eighty-nine black-eyed Susan's for her birthday, followed by two living black-eyed Susan plants that she could enjoy all summer long. By the way, my mother's name is Susan, so the flowers had a special significance to her. We're planning to send her ninety roses next year, since roses are her favorite flower.

Carol, Florida

❧ *The Best Gift I Ever Got* ❧

When I turned sixteen, my birthday present from my mother was a certificate for an introductory flight lesson. That one lesson opened up the world of aviation to me. I went on to get my commercial, instrument, and multiengine ratings and continue to fly today—some thirty years later.

Betsy, Florida

Gifts for Teenagers

These young adults are a tough crowd to please in everyday life so finding the perfect present for a perennially picky teen can be quite a challenge. Teens are so tuned in to the latest fads and crazes that a totally cool gift you buy in March for an April birthday may be old news by the time the party rolls around. That's why I believe your best bet when buying for teenagers is a gift certificate from a brick-and-mortar or online store where you know they'll find something they like. Good places to consider include Target, Tower Records, and Blockbuster video stores, all of which sell gift cards in a variety of denominations.

❧ *The Best Gift I Ever Gave* ❧

For my boyfriend's birthday, I bought him a hiking backpack to match the one I used whenever we went backpacking. This pack has ten pockets, and I filled each of them with a different gift. In one, I put a CD that he wanted; in another, a printout of three super-8 cameras I'd ordered for him on eBay. There was also a guidebook to Cuba, since we were going there in a week. Each time he found another gift in the pocket, he was shocked and more grateful. I continued the tradition the next year with a new bag, but this time, I put in each pocket something he'd lost over the past year (but that I found or repurchased for him). The stuff included his favorite Gap baseball hat and a new wallet.

Heidi, New York

Here's one reason I believe this approach works best with teenagers. I have a teenage half brother that I don't see often, so I don't know his likes and dislikes very well. When I give him a birthday gift, I want it to be something he'll use and enjoy. A few years ago, I decided on a gift certificate to Amazon.com, which elicited the most enthusiastic thank-you note I'd ever received from a relative, let alone a teen. So, the next birthday, I repeated the gift. This past summer, I happened to see my half brother shortly before his birthday and told him that I wasn't sure if he'd want to get the Amazon.com gift certificate yet again. "Are you kidding?" he said. "I love that gift. It's the best." Based on that response, I'll probably continue to buy him that gift certificate until he's in his twenties—or until I ask him again in a few years if he still likes that gift, and he gives me a different response.

Gifts for Adults

Once we reach our adult years, it becomes harder and harder to justify giving each other more "stuff." I speak as a homeowner whose garage and basement are both overflowing with "stuff"—and which stuff I'm slowly starting to put up for sale on eBay. But that's fodder for another book. I bring up the issue of "stuff" for a simple reason: it's why you want to target your adult gift-giving toward something you're confident the recipient will like and use, as opposed to something he or she will just store, along with the other useless stuff, in the basement or garage. Case in point: the bird-related gifts I tend to give my mother, because I know that bird-watching continues to be one of her hobbies.

Here's another example of how hobbies can tell you a lot about potential gifts for someone—and help you to avoid just giving "stuff." A woman I know has a sister who is an obsessed garage sale-goer. She's a creative person who knows how to turn other people's castoffs into personal treasures. Each weekend, she's out scouting her local area for sales. For a few birthdays running, my friend has given her sister something that she could use on her treks. One year, it was a laminated, spiral-bound atlas of her area, since the foldout map she'd been using to locate garage sales was worn out and starting to tear. The next year, she bought a nifty spill-proof travel mug so her sister could get her caffeine fix in transit and not have to worry about spilling her coffee all over the place. The bargain hunter has used each of these gifts with enthusiasm, because the giver chose them to complement her passion. Do you have to buy a gift for someone with an obvious pastime or hobby? Can you find some sort of gift that will help this person pursue this favorite past time or hobby? If so, then you've found a great gift.

❧ *The Best Gift I Ever Got* ❦

I've always loved giraffes. For my forty-fifth birthday, my husband asked me to meet him for lunch—and at the zoo, of all places. I was a little surprised but open to the possibilities. It turned out that he'd arranged for me to have a private audience with the zoo's giraffe. I got to stand right next to the giraffe, pat it, and feed it bananas. (You have no idea how long a giraffe's tongue is until you get up close and personal.) My husband took a picture of the giraffe and me, and I treasure that picture—as well as that birthday gift.

Carolyn, Ohio

❧ *The Best Gift I Ever Gave* ❦

Before we were married, my husband, Todd, was living in Texas, and I was living in New Jersey. Every time I talked to him, he raved about an Austin restaurant called The Salt Lick, which makes out-of-this-world barbeque. Years later, I discovered that The Salt Lick had opened a mail-order business. With Todd's birthday around the corner (he was with me in New Jersey by now), I decided to order him dinner from The Salt Lick as his gift. It arrived on his birthday in a cooler of dry ice, and he told me it was the best and most unexpected gift he'd ever received. This one package of food ended up giving us ten delicious dinners.

Jeannine, California

Of course, not every person to whom you'll be giving a birthday gift is obvious about his or her likes, dislikes, and hobbies. That's why a gift certificate from a retailer along the lines of Target or Amazon.com, where there's something for everyone, should do in a pinch. I know a lot of people think that gift certificates or gift cards are too impersonal. Well, to those detractors I say, "Feh." Which is better? Not buying anything because your paralyzed by indecision? Or getting a potentially impersonal gift card, which is a gift nonetheless?

Overall, the most challenging adults to buy for are parents or grandparents. My first line of defense is always to ask the person what he or she would like. However, I realize that parents can sometimes give you an answer like "Oh, honey, I don't need anything. I have everything I'd ever want," which can send you screaming to the shrink—not to mention throw a wrench into your gift-buying works. But don't let this response lead you to avoid gift giving altogether. I believe that you must always remember your parents or grandparents on their birthdays, even if it's just with a bouquet of flowers delivered from the local florist. For more pizzazz, buy them something that they would never get for themselves—an expensive bottle of wine that your dad can use to toast his birthday or a gift certificate from a local nail salon so that your grandmother can treat herself to a pedicure.

Of course, an all-time favorite gift for parents and grandparents is a nicely framed photograph of you or, even better if you have them, your kids. I've yet to see a parent or grandparent who didn't wax sentimental when presented with a picture of their offspring or their offspring's offspring. You can expand the photo idea a bit and do a picture of you and the kids on a mug or sweatshirt. Grandparents love this kind of stuff.

5

THE BUSINESS OF GIVING BUSINESS GIFTS

I learned firsthand what makes an outstanding business gift many years ago when I was working as an assistant at a magazine in New York City. I worked for two executives, and that first holiday, they both gave me gifts that went above and beyond the ordinary in my mind. One was a silver-plated pen from Tiffany, and the other was a gift certificate for a half day at Georgette Klinger, an upscale spa. Those gifts were so timeless and classic that even though I received them more than a decade ago, I'd give either of them in a second to a colleague or employee today.

What makes a pen and a gift certificate so extraordinary? First, the pen was from the venerable institution Tiffany & Company. It was a beautiful pen, and I thought of my boss's generosity each time I used it to sign his correspondence and my own. But what made the gift so memorable is what happened when he handed it to me. It was the first time anyone had ever given me anything from Tiffany, so receiving the trademark robin's egg blue box tied with a satiny white ribbon literally made me gasp, and I broke into a broad smile. It didn't matter to me what was inside; I was just so pleased that someone had bought me something from Tiffany. I've since received many gifts from Tiffany, and I still get excited each time someone gives me one of those gorgeous blue boxes. That's why Tiffany continues to be my favorite store from which to buy (or receive) business gifts.

The gift certificate meant a lot for a different reason. My boss recognized that as a young person just out of college, I couldn't afford to pamper myself with spa treatments. She knew that a little indulgence now and again could do wonders for a person's outlook as well as her appearance. In addition, she knew that I looked up to her as a mentor, and I believe she chose this spa because she went there herself. Not only could she vouch for the quality of the services, but also it was her way of letting me feel just like her for a few hours. After Christmas, I made an appointment for a facial, manicure, and pedicure (my first all-around), and when I walked out of the spa, I was on cloud nine.

That year, I wrote two of the most heartfelt thank-you notes of my professional career.

Small Business Gifts

Corporate gift giving isn't for big businesses only. Plenty of entrepreneurs and owners of small businesses engage in a gift exchange at the holidays. Here are some statistics from a recent American Express Small Business Gift-Buying Survey:

- More than three million small business owners buy corporate gifts each year, spending on average about $1,800 for these gifts.

- Employees are the most often cited recipients, followed by clients and vendors.

- The best way to make sure your employees and clients enjoy your gift? Feed them. Food is one of the most popular gifts. Money and, believe it or not, office supplies are perennial favorites as well.

- Gift giving isn't just being nice; it's good business. Of the owners surveyed, 78 percent said that holiday gift giving has helped to improve business; 71 percent said that gift giving is an important part of the company's marketing plan; and 84 percent reported that giving employees a holiday gift helped to boost morale.

❧ The Best Gift I Ever Gave ❧

In the past, I've puzzled about a good gift to give clients. I knew I wanted to give some sort of gift basket, but I wasn't sure which kind. Then I discovered Wolferman's, a Kansas company that is known for its gourmet English muffins, scones, marmalade, coffees, and teas. I love sending them because they are distinctive and because I feel as if I'm treating the office to a morning coffee break.

Margie, Massachusetts

Best Bets for Business Gifts

So, now you know that I like packages from Tiffany and gift certificates for pampering. While the examples I've cited were holiday gifts, the rules for what's appropriate to give in a business setting apply for all gift-giving occasions that might occur at work—birthdays, promotions, or the birth or adoption of a child. Here are some ideas to keep in mind as you make your corporate gift-giving decisions.

Buy from Upscale Retailers

One more time: as far as I'm concerned, anything that comes in a blue Tiffany box is money well spent. That's because the value of a gift from Tiffany is magnified by the experience of opening it. The same can be said for gifts from other well-known institutions that have either familiar packaging (think gold box from Godiva) or a name that people automatically associate with high quality, such as Saks Fifth Avenue, Neiman Marcus, Nordstrom or Crate & Barrel. Also worthy of this category: a boutique in your town that everyone recognizes as top of the line.

Treat Someone to a Service

Because I could never have afforded to splurge on a spa treatment for myself, my boss's gift meant that much more to me. Years later, I gave a gift certificate for a manicure to each of the women who worked at the day care center that my daughters attended. Think first of anything pampering-related when you want a wonderful gift for support staff. Another possibility is gift certificates from restaurants in your area where you've eaten and you're confident your secretary or office mate would enjoy having a meal. Or, if you know that your client or colleague frequents a specific spa, buy a gift certificate for a treatment there.

Food Has Mass Appeal

Currently, the gift I give all of my corporate clients is a box of chocolate truffles from Harry and David. I reason that most people would never buy themselves a box of chocolates to indulge in, so I do it for them. The main appeal of giving chocolates is that they're appropriate across the corporate spectrum—from your company's receptionist to the president and CEO of a major corporation.

Other ideas to consider in the food category include fruit baskets and sweet treats, such as cookies and brownies. The bonus to giving food is that the recipient can share the gift with coworkers or family, which lets you both spread the cheer. Of course, if the person avoids certain foods because of health or religious reasons, you'll need to take that into account. For example, I have one client with diabetes, so instead of sending food, I send flowers.

❧ *The Best Gift I Ever Got* ❧

A client of mine sent me a box of chocolate truffles for Christmas one year, which arrived on the same day that we found out there would likely be layoffs in the near future. That box of chocolates was the perfect pick-me up for a very gloomy day at the office.

Kay, California

Greenery Is Good

Another universal gift for a client or staff member is a bouquet of fresh-cut flowers. I don't know a soul who doesn't brighten at the receipt of fresh blooms. If a bouquet would convey the wrong sentiment, such as a male boss sending a female colleague flowers, order up a more conservative potted plant; for holidays, these would include seasonal flowers such as a poinsettia or Christmas cactus, or a lily for Easter.

Stay Within Bounds

Generally speaking, there's nothing wrong with giving a personalized business gift that pertains to the recipient's hobby. For example, I know a businessperson who gave a horseback riding-loving client a coffee-table book on Thoroughbreds. However, you have to tread carefully when you enter this territory. Why? Because some seemingly utilitarian gifts may violate a company policy and cause the recipient trouble. A case in point is a company that strictly forbids alcohol on the premises: while a bottle of wine may seem like a good choice for the person you know who collect vintage vintages, under these circumstances it could blow up in your face—or the recipient's. Also avoid any gifts that could be interpreted as sexual in any respect. You don't want a holiday or birthday gift to result in your getting slapped with a sexual harassment suit. Lingerie may seem like the ideal gift for a woman associate, but even a gift certificate to a lingerie store—no matter how much the person may like it—can have the wrong connotations. Don't give anyone the slightest reason to misinterpret your message.

Gifts Going to Other Countries

With today's global economy, you may well have to send a gift to a business colleague or client in another country. While the gift-giving rules in English-speaking countries such as Canada, the United Kingdom, and Australia tend to resemble those in the United States, the customs in some other places around the globe could render your well-meaning gift an insult or, worse, a death wish. Following are some of pointers on giving gifts to an international clientele.

Colors Have Certain Connotations

You might have noticed that Asian brides wear bright red wedding dresses, but did you know why? White is considered to be the color of death in Asian countries such as China, Korea, and Vietnam, thus the colorful wedding attire. Black has the same connotation, and that's why, regardless of what you buy an Asian business associate, you should never present it in a black-and-white box. Red is the color of happiness and is always a good choice for gift packaging, if not for the gift itself.

There are a number of other ways a certain color can trip you up. For example, in the United States, sending someone yellow roses signifies friendship, but in certain European countries, including France, Spain, and Germany, yellow roses mean anything but friendship. In France, for instance, yellow is the color of infidelity. In Spain, yellow and white flowers are sent when someone dies. That means that if you really must send a European colleague flowers, avoid those that are either yellow or white.

In other parts of the world, the colors blue and white are verboten. Because in the Arab world, Israel is seen as a universal enemy, you would want to avoid giving a colleague of Arab descent anything having to do or representative of Israel, including something featuring the colors blue and white (which are the same colors of the Israeli flag).

Timepieces Are Taboo

Like the color white, for many Asians timepieces such as clocks and watches have a death connotation—perhaps precisely because they show the passing of time. While Asians have clocks in their homes and offices, and they wear watches just as Americans do, do not give an Asian person a timepiece as a gift.

Knives of Any Kind Can Give Offense

To an American, a letter opener is a benign corporate gift. To a person of Asian descent, this is not so. The same caveat holds for a set of knives as a wedding gift for a business associate. That's because knives and other cutting instruments often represent tools of suicide in Asian communities. People in Latin America and the Middle East may attach similar meanings to knives, so ban anything bladed from your business gift list.

Go for Substance

Regardless of how much you spend on a business gift, if it doesn't seem substantial, it won't be well received by a client overseas. People in Europe, Asia, Latin America, and elsewhere tend to be very status-conscious—even more so than Americans—so a gift from a company with a recognizable and revered name, such as Tiffany or Godiva, is always welcomed. If you're going to give a pen, for instance, you'll make the strongest impression if it's from a well-known manufacturer such as Montblanc or Waterman. Think big when giving name-brand gifts and make sure that the company or manufacturer has an overall upscale image if you want to gift to impress.

❧ The Best Gift I Ever Got ❧

When I was a fashion editor in New York, I was always getting flowers and wine as gifts. One year a public relations person with whom I'd worked sent me three current books on fashion, all of them coffee-table style. It was a unique gift that I enjoyed so much that I actually read each from cover to cover.

Kathleen, Pennsylvania

Read Labels

Let's say you're congratulating yourself on finding the just-right gift for your colleague in China. It's from a well-known store (as I suggest above), and it seems to be good quality, but when you happen to turn it over and read the label, you see that it was made somewhere other than the United States. What should you do? Take it back. People around the globe are often more label-conscious than

Americans and don't want to receive a gift that was made in their own backyard or, worse, a place where merchandise is mass-produced. To maintain goodwill, you're wise to buy items that are made in the U.S.A. or other countries with special appeal, such as Ireland for crystal or France for wine.

If you can't tell where a gift you're considering buying was made, ask. If the salesperson doesn't give you a satisfactory answer, shop elsewhere. If you want to remove the uncertainty from your shopping, do business with retailers that understand the importance of identifying a product's origin. For example, the L.L.Bean corporate sales catalog specifies which products are made in America (sometimes denoting if a product was made right in New England, where the company is headquartered) and which are imported.

Chocolates Are (Almost) Always a Good Choice

If there's one gift that is globally accepted, it's boxed chocolates—for many of the reasons previously mentioned. They're an indulgence that most people wouldn't buy for themselves, they're a tasty treat, and they can be shared with family or colleagues. In addition, many varieties bear the stamp of an upscale retailer and are American-made products. However, there is a wrinkle in chocolate's perfection: don't send them to people in countries known for their own chocolate industry, such as Switzerland, Belgium, and France. Doing so could be seen as an insult—as if their country's own chocolates aren't good enough.

The Key to Key Chains

Since businesspeople worldwide carry keys—to their homes, offices, cars,—key chains are always a safe gift. Give it distinction by purchasing the accessory from a store with distinction, such as Tiffany, so that the item will seem substantial to the recipient.

Go With Upscale Liquors

Unlike in the American workplace, liquor isn't such a taboo in many offices overseas. If you'd like to send some spirits—either distilled or fermented—to one of those offices, do it with class by selecting a top-shelf brand such as Chivas Regal or Glenlivet. Or send a local product distinct to your area of the country. For example, if you're based in the Silicon Valley and you want to send a bottle of wine to a foreign colleague, choose one from a vineyard near to your own backyard, such as Napa or Sonoma for the Northern California gift giver.

Consider the Clients Culture

There are certain idiosyncrasies to keep in mind when giving gifts to certain cultures. Here are some to consider:

* While an upscale liquor would be eminently suitable for a typical Japanese client, it would be objectionable to another client elsewhere in Asia—specifically in Islamic countries where alcohol is a no-no.

* You face a different kind of prohibition in countries where the Hindu religion prevails: anything that is made from leather is a sacrilege, since cows are holy to Hindus.

* For many Asians, certain numerical combinations represent bad luck. Anything in groups of four is verboten. So, if you're going to give serving pieces to a client of Asian descent, such as glasses or coasters, don't give sets of four, eight, or twelve, as is the custom in the United States. Instead, go with five.

* As for glassware, the Asian culture holds anything having to do with light as being good, so a cut crystal vase or a mirror is a good choice.

Brush Up on International Etiquette

If your travel schedule allows, you may want to present the gift to your foreign colleague in person. Get off on the right foot by minding these rules of etiquette:

Watch Your Hands

In many Asian countries, it is polite to pass an object to someone with both hands. In an Islamic country, use only your right; using the left hand is bad manners because it is associated with tending to one's personal hygiene. Also, often a male presenting a gift to a female, or vice versa, should not touch the woman, let alone kiss her on the cheek. That's because the religion or culture may prohibit any physical exchange between people of the opposite sex who are not married to each other.

Charitable Gifts

Making a donation to a good cause can be a worthy business gift. I know a business owner who finds out what charitable organizations her clients support, and then at holiday time, she makes a donation in the client's name. When she sends a holiday card she encloses a note letting the person know of the contribution she's made in lieu of a traditional holiday gift.

Refusal Is Acceptance

If you were to offer a gift to an American and the person refused to accept it, you'd probably utter "Oh, OK" and put the gift away. But in some foreign cultures, refusing a gift is actually a way of being polite. So, if you present a gift to someone and are rebuffed, offer it again. Let the person know that it was no trouble to buy this gift (even if it was), and persist until you're successful. It may take a couple of times back and forth of you offering and the would-be recipient refusing, but this is just part of being polite in certain cultures.

Gifts Are Opened in Privacy

Another surprise to many Americans is that in some cultures, people don't open gifts in front of the giver. If you present a gift to someone who puts it away unopened, accept that this is the way things are done and that the recipient is just being polite, according to local custom. Likewise, if your gift does not elicit a gush of thank-yous, don't be dismayed. In many cultures, it is rude to thank a gift giver repeatedly.

~ 6 ~

How-tos for the Holiday Season

It's easy for me to get in a gift-giving mood at holiday time. Unbridled commercialism notwithstanding, it's a time to show people that you care for them. While the holidays can be exhausting, the look on a friend's face when he or she pulls open that bow makes all the work and stress of shopping worth it. Even though I'm an expert on this, I don't give what would be considered extravagant gifts. Instead, I've become a pro at zeroing in on things that people really want or will really use, which is the secret of gift-giving cheer.

Holiday Gift-Planning Tips

This past Christmas, we gave our neighbors poinsettias—a common holiday token—but I was able to turn a conventional gift into one that was unique and affordable and that truly conveyed a message of caring. Here's what I did—and what you can do, too, when planning holiday gift-giving to neighbors and friends.

Plan Ahead

I ordered the poinsettias from my daughters' school in October, when most people were thinking Halloween, not Christmas. The school was running a poinsettia fund-raiser that promised not only attractive prices but also plants in a variety of color combinations that you couldn't find at the local florist. We ordered some plants with peppermint-striped leaves, some with leaves the color of pink cotton candy, as well as cherry red and snow white ones. All told, I probably spent $50. The plants arrived in early December looking vibrant and fresh.

❧ *The Best Gift I Ever Gave* ❧

The best gift I ever gave my parents was one of the simplest: a calendar you get at a quick-copy place that has a different photo that you provide for each month of the year. I dug way back into pictures from my childhood and enlisted my sister's help in finding the most meaningful images to match each month. For example, for the month of my parents' wedding anniversary, I used a shot of them on their wedding day. For December, I selected a really neat family photo in front of the Christmas tree from thirty years ago. Tears welled in their eyes as they flipped through the pages and recalled all those memories. That was years ago, and my mother still has that calendar on her refrigerator; she turns the page each month for the sake of the picture, not the calendar itself.

Therese, California

❧ *The Best Gift I Ever Gave* ❧

When our daughter was five, she had to have heart surgery in mid-December. In the hospital, she asked Santa to bring her a playhouse for Christmas. She'd been through so much that we were determined to make her wish come true, so we arranged to have a playhouse built in our backyard in time for Christmas. The look on her face on Christmas morning, when she came home from the hospital, was worth every penny we'd spent on the playhouse.

Miriam, California

Enlist Your Children

In my opinion, there's nothing as touching as a young child presenting you with a holiday gift. Regardless of the object itself, you can't help but turn to mush when a sweet young voice says "Merry Christmas" or "Happy Chanukah." So, on a Sunday two weeks before Christmas, we rolled out my daughters' fire engine-red wagon from the garage and loaded it up with the poinsettias. Then we walked from house to house making deliveries. I had one daughter ring the doorbell and the other hold the plant. They called out "Merry Christmas" in concert, as if on cue. Our good timing also meant that no one was yet frantically rushing to stores to accomplish last-minute shopping—everyone was at home to receive our cheer. What helped make the moment even more magical was the fact that we were experiencing our first snow of the year (which I realize would be impossible for you to accomplish if you live in a warm climate).

Most Popular Gifts

People cluster around certain gift categories when doing their holiday shopping. Here are some of the most popular holiday gift purchases:

1. Clothing (60 percent)
2. Gift cards, gift certificates and money (43 percent)
3. Entertainment items, such as books, tapes, CDs, and movies (42 percent)
4. Toys and games (37 percent)
5. Books, magazines, and magazine subscriptions (35 percent)
6. Electronics and appliances (33 percent)
7. Perfume, cologne, and cosmetics (31 percent)
8. Home furnishings and decorative items (24 percent)

Timing Really Is Everything

By choosing mid-December to distribute our good cheer, we were able to reach our neighbors when they were still excited about the holidays. That weekend, most people we visited were either draping their homes with lights, bringing out their ornaments, or getting ready to go out and buy a tree. They weren't worn out from holiday shopping, cooking, or planning, which made them more receptive.

Many of us have friends and relatives whom we see only during Christmas or Chanukah, so we're inevitably giving them gifts when they're already surrounded by gifts. If you want to make your effort ring out, try to plan your presentation for a unique time, as I did with the mid-December weekend.

Gift-Giving Basics

I estimate that I've purchased nearly one thousand gifts during my tenure as a gift-giving expert—and hundreds more over my lifetime. In the process, I've noted an interesting phenomenon: among all the gift-giving occasions throughout the year, buying gifts for Christmas, Chanukah, or whatever winter holiday people celebrate, causes the most anxiety. The gifts that people give at this particular time seem to have the most importance. Perhaps that's because the holidays are often the one time of the year when an entire family gets together, and everyone wants to make a good impression. Or maybe it's a societal thing, compounded by heavy-handed advertising that almost paralyzes people about their gift-giving decisions.

> ### ❧ *The Best Gift I Ever Got* ❦
>
> For me, the most meaningful gift is jewelry. When you wear that piece of jewelry, you automatically think of that person. For example, on Christmas, my daughter gave me a pair of gold earrings with a beautiful blue stone in them. They were the first piece of jewelry she'd ever given me. I love wearing them, and I always think of her whenever I do.
>
> *Judy, Maine*

When I speak to groups across the country about gift giving, I hear the same question echoed: What am I going to buy my mother/sister/husband for the holidays? I know why people continually ask me this question: they wonder how they can continue to come up with original ideas for people to whom they give gifts year after year. Well, dear gift giver, do not worry. Over time, I've developed a sure-fire way of putting together great holiday gifts, and I'd like to share some my basics with you.

Make a List

Jewish, Christian, Muslim, or any other religion, we can all take a tip from Santa. That is, when it comes to holiday shopping, make a list and check it twice. Or simply keep a running list of everyone to whom you intend to give something. Allow yourself a few days to accomplish this task, as names may come to you in the shower or during your commute to work, and it's best to compile all your names in one list before you set out on the hunt for the perfect present. This exercise in list-making will help you in several ways:

- *It gets you organized.* Once you see who is on your naughty-or-nice list, you can begin to organize your shopping efforts. You can determine what you want to buy for whom, and then plan your store visits (or logging onto e-tailers) accordingly.

- *It keeps you focused.* With my holiday gift list in hand this past year, I was able to streamline my shopping so that I had to visit only four stores (or the websites of those stores) to accomplish all of my gift buying. My stores of choice this year were Target, Best Buy, Barnes and Noble, and Harry and David.

- *It helps you stay within budget.* When you've got a plan of attack for your holiday acquisitions, you're much less likely to wind up in a shopping frenzy. If you've identified the CD you want to buy for your brother or the kitchen appliance that suits your aunt to a T—and you've planned for the purchase financially—you're likely to come away from your holiday shopping with your spending under control.

❧ *The Best Gift I Ever Got* ☙

I got a ten-speed bike for Christmas when I was sixteen. I had been begging for one for about three years, so when I finally got it, I was thrilled. I eventually got rid of the bike last year when we moved—about twenty-seven years after I'd received it. It meant that much to me.

Therese, California

Get Personal

Whenever possible, I like to choose a gift related to the recipient's hobby—something that helps the person enjoy his or her free time more fully. For example, as I've mentioned, I grew up in a home where referencing a field guide to birds was as common as looking up a phone number in the yellow pages. A few years ago my mother retired to Maine, where bird-watching has become an even bigger part of her day. So, I've adjusted my gift giving for her birthday and Christmas to reflect her expanding devotion to her hobby. Last year, we bought her a squirrel-proof bird feeder from L.L.Bean. This year, I've already got her two new books about birds. One is an updated field guide to replace the dog-eared version that she's had for ages; the other is a coffee-table book on birds from the Audubon Society (of which she's a member). Next year I'm sure I'll figure out something else bird-related for her gift.

When you draw a blank on what to buy for someone—let's say, your brother-in-law—ask yourself: What does this person like to do in his free time? What are some of his hobbies? What activity do I hear him talking about? Once you have this profile, you'll know which way to head. For example, if you need to buy a gift for someone who subscribes to *The Wine Spectator* and is always on the lookout for an intriguing vintage, anything wine-related would be fitting. I've seen some stunning hand-blown glass bottle stoppers that replace a cork once the wine is opened. These stoppers do double duty as a functional item and an objet d'art. Other wine-related gifts include sturdy but beautiful goblets and nifty wine racks. Given that I know my own brother-in-law is an oenophile (a fancy work for a wine lover), these are all gifts I would consider giving to him—and have in the past!

Ask Questions

One of the biggest mistakes people make when approaching gift giving is to assume that the inspiration for the perfect gift will come to them out of thin air. Nothing could be further from the truth. I always say that being a good gift giver is a lot like being a journalist: you need to be observant, and you can't be afraid to ask questions. You can sniff out the recipient's likes and dislikes with indirect queries such as "Are you doing any new hobbies these days?" or "What do you think of the new CD by (you fill in the blank)?" If the answers don't yield any gift-giving insight, then bite the bullet and ask straight out, "What would you like for the holidays?"

If you get the common (and utterly frustrating) response "Oh, I don't need anything," don't back down. Let your friends and family members know that you're looking forward to buying them something as a holiday gift and that you don't want to burden them with having to return this gift if it's not something they'll like. They may as well save themselves the trouble and suggest some gift ideas. Get them thinking by asking if there's anything they saw in a magazine, on television, or in a store that appealed to them but that they couldn't justify buying. Prod them about a friend who may have some trinket or tool that they'd like to have as well. When you gently but firmly nudge them along, you'll gather the input you need.

❧ The Best Gift I Ever Gave ❧

At my parents' house a few years ago, I came across a huge box filled with old family movies. These films dated back to the 1950s, when I was a kid. Over the next couple of weekends, my husband and I organized the more than one hundred reels in chronological order and spliced them together as a single reel. On Christmas day, we pulled out my dad's old film projector, loaded the reel, and sat back in delight as my parents watched the movie of their life together. It was a wonderful gift to give.

Leslie, New York

Don't Reinvent the Wheel

I said it in the Introduction, and I reiterate it here. When you find a gift that the recipient clearly enjoys, go right ahead and give it again in following years—that is, until the recipient asks you to stop or, if it's a young person, until the gift is no longer appropriate. I strongly endorse not messing with success when it comes to gifts.

My mother gives my husband The Home Depot gift cards every Christmas. She's been doing this for years, and I hope she'll continue to do so. My husband has come to expect this gift, and it's a gift that makes him happier than any seemingly more "personal" gift would. That's because to my husband, a self-professed handyman, The Home Depot is his shopping mecca. Receiving a gift card gives him carte blanche to go shopping for his wood shop, and that makes him utterly happy. What more could you want from a gift?

> ### → *The Best Gift I Ever Gave* ←
>
> I gave my baby-sitter what I think is the best holiday gift: a night out
> with her husband. Inside of a handwritten card, I put two passes to the
> local movie theater, a gift certificate from a nearby restaurant that I
> know she loves, and a handmade coupon that said I would watch her
> kids on whatever night she wanted to go out to the movies.
>
> *Carrie, Wisconsin*

Likewise, as I disclosed in the previous chapter, I've adopted the practice of sending my business associates and corporate clients Harry and David truffles for the holidays. These yummy chocolates have proved to be a welcome antidote to the craziness that plagues businesses during December, and I hear time and again how much people enjoy receiving them—and polishing them off. Until the overwhelming response from my clients is *against* getting chocolates, I'll stay the course.

Finally, my brother-in-law struck gold with a gift for me a few years ago—a pair of earrings from a one-of-a-kind jewelry shop in New York City. They were like nothing I'd ever seen before—a dangling ruby surrounded by two tiny pearls—and I wore them almost every day that year. Before the next Christmas, my brother-in-law asked me what I wanted, and I told him, fingering my favorite earrings (which I was wearing, of course), "Another pair of earrings from that store, please." He obliged, and every Christmas since then, he's given me earrings from this fabulous shop. Every Christmas, I can't wait to open my little box of jewelry from my brother-in-law.

Shopping for Toddlers to Teens

My recommendations on buying holiday gifts for children are much the same as those outlined previously on buying birthday gifts. Here is a rundown of ways to find lots of age-appropriate gifts.

Gifts for Babies

The most important quality to look for in a toy for a baby is safety. Refer to the Consumer Products Safety Commission website (cpsc.gov) for guidelines on safe toys. Then, once you know they're safe, focus on toys that promote early-stage development—ones with handles for small fingers to grab onto or toys that make noise when shaken. Books are also an answer to the question of what to give a small child. I would think that every parent would cherish receiving a book as a gift for his or her child—I know that I do.

❧ *The Best Gift I Ever Got* ❧

When my family moved from the United States to Okinawa, Japan, in the 1980s, we enjoyed the fresh pineapples and other tropical fruits, but we dyed-in-the-wool New Englanders craved McIntosh apples. One Christmas, my sister, who was living in Massachusetts at the time, went out and picked two dozen McIntosh apples and had them shipped to us. Not only were these twenty-four apples rationed like water on a drifting life raft, but also we kept the shipping box in the living room for weeks afterward so the aroma of the apples would permeate the house.

Laura, Massachusetts

Gifts for Toddlers and Preschoolers

Because children this age are in high gear, toys for running, pushing, and building are a good fit. In addition to physical mobility, this is a time when a young child's imagination begins to explode, so a gift that helps the child harness her mental energy—such as dress-up clothes or a plastic tea-party set—would be prized.

Gifts for Kids in Elementary School

As kids get older and more sophisticated, so too should the toys you buy them. Now is the time to get a board game that the child can play with friends or family, such as Candy Land, Chutes and Ladders, Twister, or my daughters' new favorite, Don't Wake Daddy. If the child is familiar with computers, as more and more young children are, you can offer a fun, educational CD-ROM game or "living book." At the same time, simple playground toys that encourage outdoor activities or creative play, such as a jump rope, sidewalk chalk or a set of balls, are also great for active kids on your gift list.

> ### ❧ *The Best Gift I Ever Got* ❧
>
> I've always loved the smell of real Christmas trees, but when I was grow-
> ing up, my family used an artificial tree every year. One winter day, I was
> talking to a high school friend about how much I missed the evergreen
> smell of a genuine Christmas tree. Well, the next day, he came over with
> a small, real tree, already decorated with bows and lights. It was just the
> right size for me to keep in my bedroom, and I enjoyed that piney aroma
> every night as I drifted off to sleep.
>
> *Nicole, Mississippi*

Giving Kids Gifts with Safety in Mind

According to the National Safe Kids Campaign, an organization dedicated to the pre-
vention of childhood injury, you should keep the following safety ideas in mind when
shopping for children's gifts:

- Only children over age three should receive toys with small, removable parts—
  they are a choking hazard for younger tots. To verify that a toy is age-appropriate, check the box. Most toy manufacturers label toys that are inappropriate for
  kids under age three. If you're buying the toy online, make sure the website
  offers this safety information.

- Be aware of toys that could hurt children in other ways, such as those with sharp
  points or edges, which can cut a child, or those that make a loud noise and may
  damage hearing.

- Make sure that any string, strap, or cord attached to the toy is no longer than
  seven inches. Otherwise, it could strangle a child.

- Reserve electrical toys for kids over age eight. If the toy has a battery compartment, the compartment ideally should be kept shut with a screw, to help reduce
  the risk of burns.

- If you give a toy with wheels—such as a bike, a scooter, or skates—accompany it
  with protective gear. Nearly half a million kids visit emergency rooms each year
  because of accidents related to bicycles, skateboards, in-line skates, and roller
  skates. Such gear could include a helmet, kneepads, elbow pads, wrist guards,
  reflective stickers, and a horn or bell. Also, when it comes to in-line skates, one of

the hardest parts of learning to use them is figuring out how to stop. Therefore, a certificate for a few introductory lessons would make a great add-on.

For more information on safe toys, visit the organization's website at safekids.org.

Gifts for Teenagers

Try as one may, teens can be a challenge for conscientious gift givers. No matter how hip you think you are because you watch MTV every once in a while, unless you live and breathe the teen world, the smart money says you are totally out of touch with what's in and what's out. It's this honesty that leads me to again proclaim that the best gift for a teen is a gift certificate or gift card from a store whose depths are certain to contain something that he or she would like. Some of my favorite places to get a gift certificate for a teen include Target, Tower Records, Barnes and Noble, and Amazon.com. Another gift idea to consider along the same lines: a gift card to iTunes.com, the website and online store where you can shop for downloadable songs for a computer or an iPod. How hip will you seem if you give a gift to a teen that's downloadable!

Intelligence Gathering

Whenever you're feeling out of the loop about what to give a child, do some basic reconnaissance. Call the parents for a briefing on what the child likes to do or any hobbies the child has. If you're comfortable asking, inquire about any specific gift suggestions or things to avoid. If you're out at a store such as Target or Toys R Us, watch kids the same age as the child for whom you're buying, and take note of the items they seem to be drawn to and what elicits the most excited reactions. If you are feeling bold, approach the accompanying fathers or mothers, explain your mission, and ask for anecdotal accounts or opinions based on their children's likes and dislikes. By surveying your target audience, you'll be sure to uncover more age-appropriate gifts than you can carry.

Gift-Giving FAQs

Q: Inevitably, I get invited to tree-trimming parties or open houses around the holidays. I know that I'm supposed to take along some sort of gift to contribute to the festivities, but I never know what to choose. Help!

A; It can be demanding to add party-hopping to your already overflowing "to do" list at the holidays, but to nurture your long-term relationships with friends, family, and neighbors, try to attend as many of these events as you can—even if it's for only an hour. These kinds of holiday get-togethers are a great way to spread holiday cheer, and—who knows?—you may bump into someone you haven't seen in a long time and rekindle your acquaintance. As for what to take, you have a few options that are easy to handle, easy to find and not too expensive.

It never hurts to ask the host, "What can I bring?" In fact, whenever I plan a holiday party, I don't spend much time agonizing over what to serve for dessert. That's because whenever people ask what they can bring (and I know that my friends and family members will), I just reply, "A dessert." If you don't get the opportunity to inquire, I doubt anyone would turn you away if you came bearing a fruit tart or a chocolate cake.

When you're invited to a tree-trimming party, your gift solution is simple: an ornament—preferably one that reflects a hobby or personal taste of the hosts. For example, when my husband and I attended a tree-trimming party last year that our music-loving friends were throwing, we presented them with ornaments related to musical instruments, including a silver G-clef and a festive snare drum. If your party hosts have kids, it's thoughtful to take a special, inexpensive ornament for any children of the hosts. Too often, we overlook children when we're a guest in someone's house, and your including them in the holiday celebration will mean a lot to both the parents and the children.

When you're a guest at someone's house for a holiday party—and you'd like to do more than just bring an ornament—I believe you would be on solid ground with any of the following three hostess gifts:

- *A bottle of wine.* For these purposes, I stock up on wines that are pleasing to most palates, such as Chardonnay or Pinot Grigio (both whites). Or you can tote a bottle of Beaujolais nouveau, a French wine that is available only during the holiday season. If alcohol could be controversial, substitute sparkling cider.

- *A plant.* A Christmas cactus, a poinsettia, or any other kind of greenery is a better option than cut flowers. Why? Your hosts are probably extremely busy tending to the party, and you don't want to hand them more work along with your fresh-cut flowers—giving flowers like these means that your host will have to stop what he's doing and start fumbling for a vase, filling it with water, and arranging the flowers when all he may want to be doing is greeting his guests. A plant is a much lower-maintenance package with the same high-quality sentiment.

- *A box of chocolates.* Here again, you don't want to add to your hosts' workload by presenting a dessert that needs a lot of legwork. A box of chocolates is perfect for passing around and sharing. And individual candies fit seamlessly into a menu. For example, your host can put them out after the meal while preparing dessert and coffee—or can choose instead to keep them for herself and enjoy them after her guests have gone home.

Q: Several members of my family have birthdays around the holidays. How can I come up with a gift for both occasions?

A: As a December birthday person myself, I think the most important thing you can do for people like me is to make sure you acknowledge both the birthday and the holiday, but do it separately. One thing that drives us December birthday people crazy is getting combination presents—"Oh, here is a little something for Christmas and your birthday." It's not our fault that we were born near Christmas or Chanukah, so you shouldn't penalize the recipient by buying one gift simply because it makes your shopping easier. Use the advice offered both here and in the birthday chapter to come up with individual gifts for both occasions. Complete the picture by wrapping the birthday gift in birthday-theme paper and the holiday gift in a holiday motif so the recipient can clearly see that your intent is to honor each occasion. Also, just because you're giving two gifts, that doesn't mean that you have to spend twice as much. You could easily build on a theme by giving related gifts that add up to what you might have spent on one combined gift. This might include a paperback bestseller and a bookstore gift card, or a bag of coffee beans and a festive mug.

Q: In my free time, I've started making crafts and selling them at local flea markets. Is it OK to make people a gift for the holidays instead of buying something from a store?

A: Absolutely, so long as the items you're giving are worlds beyond the Popsicle-stick crafts we all constructed at summer camp. If your wares are good enough that shoppers at a flea market want to buy them, then it sounds as if they would make lovely holiday gifts—and most people are charmed to receive something handcrafted. I always am.

My husband's stepmother can knit and sew with the best of them, and every year, she gives each of my daughters a handmade article of clothing. One year, she made them wool sweaters; another year, it was party dresses. The girls can't wait for their custom-made clothes from Granny each year. So, if you've got the professional touch, your handmade gift will make a fine impression, whether it's a framed photograph that you shot or a serving bowl that you threw in pottery class. Your friends and loved ones will cherish it for years to come, just as my daughters—and their parents—are pleased with the hand-knit sweaters and perfect dresses from Granny's design studio.

Q: I like the idea of giving the service people in my life a small gift for the holidays, but sometimes I think they'd appreciate having the cash more. How would I figure out how much to tip them?

A: Tipping is a tough call 365 days a year. I constantly worry that I'm tipping too well when I receive shoddy service or that I'm not tipping enough when I go out to eat or get my hair done. I alternate between giving out $20 bills to service people for the holidays and boxes of chocolates to the FedEx guy or my newspaper carrier. If you're wondering how much you should tip these kinds of folks at the holidays, here are some suggestions:

- Newspaper Delivery Person—$10 to $30
- Beauty Salon Staff—$10 to $60
- Day Care Provider—$25 to $70 each, plus a small gift from your child
- Nanny—One week's pay plus a small gift from your child
- Housekeeper/Cleaning Person—$25 to $50, or one day's pay
- Regular Baby-Sitter—One evening's pay plus a small gift from your child
- Letter Carrier—They're allowed to accept gifts worth up to $20
- UPS/FedEx-like Delivery Person—$10 to $25
- Private Garage Attendant—$10 to $25
- Building Superintendent—$20 to $75
- Doorman—$10 to $55
- Private Trash Collector—$10 to $20 each
- Personal Trainer—One workout session's pay

7

HOUSEWARMING AND HOSTESS GIFTS

Moving into a new home is right up there with marriage and the birth of a child as one of the pivotal events in a person's life. When my family and I moved into the home we built a few years ago, it felt as if our life was finally complete. After spending the previous seven years as veritable nomads—we'd moved five times to four different states—it was both soothing and invigorating to settle into a place where we could finally put down roots. As friends and family began to visit, they were gracious in bringing us housewarming gifts that, in some cases, were very attractive but also practical and, in other cases, were extremely helpful as we set up house. They ranged from a rectangular ceramic serving dish from Italy to a decorative flag for the front yard to a $200 The Home Depot card, which we used in earnest the first weekend after we received it.

Sending a housewarming gift is customary when you find out that someone close to you has bought a new house or moved into a new apartment. It's simple social etiquette that our moms taught us (or I hope she did)—and which I hope to reinforce here. The same goes for a hostess gift—you should never show up at someone's house empty-handed but instead you should bring a little something that you give to the person who invites you to dinner or to stay overnight as a guest.

Tried-and-True Gifts

If your social life is anything like mine, you're frequently invited for dinner at friends' homes, even if it's just a "come on over for pizza" event. Because of this common scenario, my husband Bill and I are often in the position of coming up with hostess gifts. To add to the comings and goings at dinnertime and the hostess gifts we need to buy, we're always stocking up on housewarming gifts. That's because so many of our friends and family members have recently built or bought a house. What we're not doing is running around town trying to find something "new" for each of these occasions. As I've asserted all along, I don't believe in reinventing the wheel every time I'm obliged to give a gift. Instead, we've identified a handful of tried-and-true housewarming and hostess gifts to which we can turn whenever we need them. Here are a few of the best ones.

Wine

A nice bottle of wine works well as both a housewarming and a hostess gift, and it's my gift of choice when I go to someone's house for dinner. An easy and effective way to approach choosing a wine is to keep your eyes and ears open for recommendations.

For example, when you dine out and are served a particularly satisfying bottle of white or red, write down all the information from the label before the waiter takes the bottle away. Don't rely on your memory or a mental image of the logo, since subtle details can make major differences in taste as well as price. Or, do as I did recently: after indulging in a particularly fine glass of wine at a restaurant, I asked our waiter for more information on the vintage. Not only did she write down the name and year, but also she included the price and where I could buy it locally.

When you identify a wine, check out your local liquor store—or the place where the recommending person suggested you look for the vintage, much as the waitress at the restaurant did for me. Don't be afraid to ask the store clerk for help in finding that wine and don't give up if you don't find it at first. However, once you do locate that wine you loved—and are sure others will enjoy receiving as a hostess gift—stock up on it. (Think gift closet, but the wine cellar variety.) Then, the next time you're invited to someone's house for dinner, you won't have to scramble for a hostess gift or run out to the store at the last minute. You can just grab one of those highly recommended bottles from your stash.

When it comes to a housewarming gift, I'd still suggest giving wine but with a twist: give a personal vintage. No, I'm not suggesting that you invest in oversize vats and start pressing your own Chianti. Rather, send a message on a bottle by ordering from a winery that will custom-design the label, and print your good wishes alongside the vintage. For example, your label might read, "From our house to yours. Congratulations. Love, John and Sue."

Here are three wineries with mail-order operations that excel at this kind of personalized gift. (Note: These companies ship to only certain areas of the country where interstate transport of alcohol is allowed, so check first before settling on mail-order wine as your housewarming gift of choice.)

❧ *The Best Gift I Ever Got* ❧

When my husband and I moved into our house, a business associate gave us a generous gift certificate from a local nursery as a housewarming gift. We bought a bunch of small fruit trees. That was five years ago. Today we have a thriving orchard of citrus, plums, and nectarines, and I continue to think about that business associate and his generosity whenever I step outside and admire those trees.

Miriam, California

Chaddsford Winery

This boutique winery, headquartered in the picturesque Brandywine Valley, near Philadelphia, offers custom labeling on four of its wines: Proprietors Reserve White, Chardonnay, Proprietors Red, and Sunset Blush. You can order full- or half-bottle sizes, with a one-case minimum. In addition to the price of the wines, Chaddsford charges around $85 for up to 150 labels. If you live in the Philadelphia region and want to taste any of the wines before ordering, you'll find tasting rooms in Peddler's Village in Bucks County and Manayunk in the city of brotherly love. The main number for Chaddsford headquarters, where you place custom-label orders, is (610) 388-6221. You can also check them out on the web at chaddsford.com.

New Hope Winery

At this Bucks County, Pennsylvania, winery, you can choose a custom label for any of its twenty-five varieties. They include reds, whites, and blushes, as well as seasonal and specialty wines, which run the gamut from red sangria to Dutch apple spice (a spiked apple cider). All orders have a one-case minimum. You can pay for a case of wine and customize all the labels to be the same for approximately $3.50 per bottle, or, for a nominal extra fee, you can vary the labels. While you can select the wine and a label design through the company's website at newhopewinery.com, a representative will finalize your order the old-fashioned way—by calling you to take credit card and shipping information. Or you can do the whole thing over the phone at (800) 592-WINE (9463).

Windsor Vineyards

Windsor holds the distinction of being the first winery to offer custom-created labels, and what makes Windsor vintages noteworthy is that they are grown and bottled in Sonoma County, in California's renowned wine country. What's also important is that your custom order can be as small as two bottles. You have forty varieties from which to choose, including classics such as cabernet and chardonnay as well as dessert wines and champagne. Call (800) 333-9987, or visit Windsor Vineyards online at windsorvineyards.com.

Housewares

We have dear friends whom we have known since high school. These friends have brought or sent us a housewarming gift each time we moved—whether it was from one New York City apartment to another or across the country. Each time, they gave us housewares of some sort. One move, it was pretty ceramic candlestick holders. Another time, it was a glass vase. For each of the last two moves (I told you we've moved a lot), they gave us a green-and-white-speckled serving bowl, part of a matched set. The first bowl, to commemorate our move to a new home in New Jersey, is oversize and round, with scalloped edges. The second bowl is shallow and square—a variation on the traditional pasta bowl. We love these serving dishes, and we keep them on display in our kitchen. When we've entertained, they've held everything from potato chips to salad to pasta. This year, we even used the square bowl for our Halloween candy.

You can see why a serving bowl of some sort makes an unbeatable housewarming gift: it performs multiple functions—from adorning a shelf to holding sweets for trick-or-treaters. This versatility makes it one of my go-to housewarming gifts. I'm partial to bowls made of ceramic, painted in bright colors, and large enough to be used for a mound of salad or spaghetti. In fact, I just picked up one to send to those friends from high school—they just moved into a new home of their own.

> ## ❧ *The Best Gift I Ever Gave* ❧
>
> Because my line of work requires that I travel to Paris a lot, I like to stock up on a certain brand of hand cream that's available only in France. I usually buy it in bulk and then give it as a hostess gift when I'm invited to someone's house. It's a refreshing alternative to the usual wine or flowers, and the fact that it comes from Paris makes it "ooh-la-la."
>
> *Donna, New Jersey*

When you're on your housewares-buying quest, here's a question to consider: Do your friends collect a certain kind of dishes or material? If so, try to find a piece that goes with the collection. For example, we're big Fiestaware fans. We're drawn to the bright colors of our set and the fact that the design is versatile and will match most anything—including the beloved green-and-white serving bowls I told you about above. We use Fiestaware for our everyday dishes and have been collecting serving pieces for the set over the years. Several family members who know of our fondness for Fiestaware chose it as a housewarming gift for us. It was exactly what we wanted and needed, and their obvious effort to reflect our tastes imparted a personal sincerity—which you want for your housewarming gift whenever possible.

Try to plan your purchases to take advantage of opportunities to build your on-hand supplies. If you travel to a place where unique housewares can be found at a good price, leave some room in your suitcase, and load up while you're there. A few years ago, I had to travel to eastern Europe for business, and I discovered before I left that glass from Poland and Hungary was well regarded in the United States. I knew I'd stumbled onto a promising source for a supply of housewarming gifts, so while I was in Warsaw, Krakow, and Budapest, I focused in on inexpensive suppliers of quality glass housewares. I ended up at one shop in Warsaw that had a dazzling assortment of brightly colored hand-blown glass vases for about three American dollars, and I bought enough to fill a large shopping bag. Later in Budapest, I came across a shop with floor-to-ceiling shelves of wine goblets reminiscent of Tiffany glass. I think I stuffed a giant suitcase with those glasses, and for about a year, I had a ready supply of first-rate housewarming gifts with the added flair of having been purchased overseas.

Gift-giving FAQ:

Q: What do you give to the hosts when you stay at their house?

A: First, let me compliment you on wanting to thank the hosts for hosting you in their home by giving them a gift. This and the thank-you note are two rules of etiquette that have slipped away from modern day life. Now, what to buy.

Fortunately, when you've been a guest in someone's home, you've had the leisure to observe how the hosts live and what objects they keep around. This inside look should be a good place to start when you decide what type of gift to send by way of thanks.

For instance, my husband and I recently stayed with friends whom I had thought of as your average coffee drinkers, but upon spending a few days with them, I discovered that they were true Java aficionados. When it came time to send them a thank-you-for-hosting-us gift, we chose something that was all about coffee. This selection included a quartet of oversize mugs of funky-painted pottery and multiple bags of premium beans. I know the gift hit the spot because they called as soon as it arrived to thank *us* for sending it.

Another time, I stayed with a work colleague in Chicago while we attended a sales meeting in the city. I learned while I was with her that she was allergic to wheat and had a heck of a time finding ingredients for cakes and cookies that she could bake and enjoy. When I returned to New York, 1 made the rounds of a few health food stores and purchased a selection of wheat-free muffin, cake, and cookie mixes, which I then tucked into an attractive basket and sent off to my colleague. The thank-you note I received from her was one of the most endearing anyone has ever written to me.

Think back on your visit at someone's home to any comments or conversations during your stay that speak to your host's likes or dislikes. Or if your visit has yet to happen, try to remember to keep your gift-giving radar on alert throughout your visit. Did your friend show interest in a book you were reading and remark that she'd been meaning to read it? Buy her a copy when you get home. Was your host planning a vacation? Purchase something fun and appropriate for the trip—maybe sunblock and a straw hat for someone heading to the tropics, or a guidebook with a colorful bookmark that pertains to the city or region.

If all your investigating does not lead you to the right gift, you can go with the vast array of housewares, notepaper, or candles that I recommend you keep stocked in your gift closet and use one of these as your hostess gift. Or you can buy a gift card to a local store where you know she'll find something that's just right for herself.

8

GIFT GIVING FOR LOVERS, MOMS, DADS, AND GRADS

This chapter takes you through some annual gift-giving occasions that aren't full-blown shopping holidays but nonetheless warrant a suggestion. They are Valentines Day, Mother's Day, and Father's Day. In addition, every spring millions of students graduate from high school and college, and chances are you'll be invited to a graduation party sometime in the near future. You won't have to pull an all-nighter in search of a grade-A gift for grads after reviewing this chapter.

You Gotta Have Heart: Valentine's Day

If you're lucky enough to have been pierced by cupid's arrow, then you know how your heart races to find the right gift for Valentine's Day. I can still remember being a single twenty-something when I found myself with a boyfriend for the first time ever on Valentine's Day. (High school boyfriends never counted as much, since I didn't have a disposable income to use when shopping for a gift.) Since I'd never been in a long-term relationship, I was clueless about what to give him. We weren't very serious at the time, so I didn't want to come off as too romantic. But I didn't want to let the day go by without any recognition whatsoever. So, what did I wind up getting him? A simple wood frame that was painted red and contained a picture of me. I figured he could put it on his desk at work or somewhere in his apartment. He seemed pleased with the gift I gave him, and I loved the cotton T-shirt with tiny red hearts all over it that he got for me. In fact, I wore it for years after we'd broken up and eventually relegated it to workout clothes when it became worn-out. A few years and holes later, I finally let it go.

❧ *The Best Gift I Ever Got* ❧

When I was newly married, I had to go on a business trip, and I happened to be away on Valentine's Day. When I arrived at my destination, an employee at the site I was visiting handed me an envelope with my name on it. Inside was a Valentine's Day card from my husband, who had gone through the trouble of sending this card ahead of time so that it would be waiting for me when I arrived

Anne, North Carolina

Put Some Zing in the Heartstring

For so many couples, Valentine's Day equals chocolates in a heart-shape box and a bouquet of red roses. Both are time-honored gifts—and ones I've been happy to receive since the first Valentine's Day with my husband. If you have your heart set on a classically romantic gift for him or her, chocolates and roses are all that. So is a candlelit dinner at a favorite restaurant, and one I would recommend for a food lover. But if you're aiming to give a Valentine's Day gift with a twist, here are some that should be a hit.

C Is for Cookie

A standout gift for your sweetie is a cookie bouquet, which is just what it sounds like: cookies arranged to resemble a bouquet of flowers. You can visit a local bakery and put the arrangement together yourself, or call in the experts. One company I frequently use is Cookies by Design, which offers a basket of oversize cookies shaped and decorated to look like red roses, or one with heart-shape cookies covered with red icing—both perfect for Valentine's Day. You can choose your design and locate a Cookies by Design franchise nearest you by visiting the company's website at cookiebouquet.com. Currently, there are 213 such shops in 43 states. Seven-cookie arrangements start at $35.

Raise a Glass

Toast your love by raising a glass of champagne to each other. But don't just pop the bubbly and drink up. Instead, put together a gift of love that contains a pair of crystal champagne flutes, a small box of chocolate-dipped strawberries or chocolate candy, and a personalized bottle of champagne. You can order the latter (technically, sparkling wine, since only the French can call this bubbly spirit champagne) from Windsor Vineyards, a Sonoma County winery that has been offering personalized labels on all of its wines since it began its mail-order operations in 1959 (see Chapter 7). There is no extra charge for the three-line personalized label. To contact Windsor Vineyards call (800) 333-9987 or go online at windsorvineyards.com.

Valentine's Day Quick Tip

Plan to shop after-Valentine's Day sales to stock up on heart-related and red-hued items at closeout prices. These can come in handy in a number ways. Children can use juvenile-looking materials for Valentine's Day gifts for their friends next year. You can put aside heart-shape picture frames for bridal shower gifts. And you can adapt anything red that you've purchased for your holiday decorating, stocking stuffing, and gift giving come next December.

❧The Best Gift I Ever Got ❦

On the first Valentine's Day after my boyfriend (now husband) and I started dating, he conspired with my then-roommate to let him into our house while I was at work. He filled my bedroom with red and white helium balloons, replaced the white light bulbs in my lamps with red ones, and left a dozen roses on my bed. On this particularly bad day, I came home from work and opened my bedroom door to find more than six dozen balloons floating inside. It was fantastic. The best part was what 1 found out later: he'd had to make six trips back and forth to the florist to transport all of the balloons in his compact car.

Gwen, New Jersey

Anything (Heart-Shape) Goes

Around Valentine's Day, stores are overflowing with all things heart-shape or featuring hearts—crystal bowls, boxes of candy, picture frames, clothing—and any one of these heart-inspired items would work well as a Valentine's Day gift. You can outfit a guy in boxer shorts with hearts on them or a gal in heart-print paja-mas. If your sweetheart is more of a jewelry person, go with a pair of heart-shape earrings or a necklace with a heart-shape charm. If your guy wears shirts with French cuffs, give him heart-shape cuff links or, if that's too over the top for him, cuff links with a ruby red center. For the pint-size set, a teacher gift that's both inexpensive and thoughtful is a heart-shape red candle. By going with the heart theme, you're sure to find a great Valentine's Day gift.

Plan a Romantic Getaway

A wonderful way to enjoy Valentine's Day together is to escape to a romantic get-away. Arrange to have someone watch your kids, if necessary, and go away for the weekend like newlyweds.

I know of one man who took his wife away on Valentine's Day but didn't tell her where they were going. He told her to pack warm-weather clothing—her first hint, since they live in a cold climate—but that was the only clue he'd offer. It wasn't until they'd arrived at Miami International Airport that she discovered they were taking a weekend cruise.

If your finances won't allow for something as extravagant as a cruise, econo-mize in romantic style by spending the weekend at a bed and breakfast or coun-try inn. If you live in a city, you can book a weekend at a downtown hotel and play tourist for a change. Order room service, sleep late, and go sight-seeing. All would surely add up to a romantic Valentine's Day gift in my book.

Have a Heart-Healthy Holiday

While a heart-shape cutout is the ultimate Valentine's Day symbol, a healthful way to present a Valentine's Day gift is with the old ticker itself in mind. Here are some heart healthy ways to celebrate:

Give and eat chocolate. Chocolate lovers worldwide rejoiced recently when med-ical studies showed that dark chocolate contains antioxidants, the cancer-fighting substance also found in fruits and vegetables. In addition, chocolate does not contain cholesterol, and the monosaturated oleic acid found in chocolate has been shown to reduce cholesterol. I hope that this information helps you to feel good about giving chocolate as a Valentine's Day gift.

Get moving. An invigorating way to celebrate Valentine's Day is to get physical with the one you love. Spend the afternoon hiking in the woods, or make a date at the local ice-skating rink, where you can glide hand-in-hand like high school sweethearts. Or you could work out your heart and help others in the process by participating in a race that benefits a good cause—ideally, alongside the people you love. Each year, several races are held on or near Valentine's Day, with the proceeds helping to fund a local charity. For example, one year, the Annual Valentine Road Race in Bradford, New Hampshire, helped to raise funds to restore a church in town. Husbands and wives along with mothers and daughters ran together. You can locate a Valentine's Day race near you by checking out the *Runner's World* magazine website at runnersworld.com, which lists a calendar of races nationwide.

*   *   *   *   *

Putting Parents First: Mother's Day and Father's Day

It's probably the same old story every year: when you think about what to give the folks for Mother's or Father's Day, you quickly arrive at flowers for her and a tie for him. Perhaps, that's because you know that your mom can't get enough flowers and your dad is always short on nifty new ties to go with his suits. Without a doubt, continue sending those splendid floral arrangements each Mother's Day and those eye-catching ties on Father's Day if that's what they like.

As I've said before, if you give a gift that is well received, don't stop. There's no reason to start from scratch with each gift-giving occasion just because you're reluctant to repeat yourself. After all, most people don't prize variety for its own sake; they want to get gifts that they'll use and enjoy. If you know that your mother or father (or a grandparent, for that matter) used and enjoyed your previous years' gifts, then don't mess with success. While you may tell yourself that you should give your parents something different, if a new and different gift is pretty to look at but not practical, it may sit in a box at the bottom of the closet—only to be brought out and displayed hours before you come over for a visit. That's not how you want people to feel about a gift you've given—that it's an obligation to accommodate. You want them to genuinely enjoy it.

If you discover that your previously loved gifts are no longer so successful, that's a different story line. Mom has developed allergies to flowers, or Dad's office has gone business casual. The easiest thing to do is apply the gift-giving strategies from previous chapters to come up with a new great idea for a Mother's Day or Father's Day gift that's sure to impress. Here's a brief recap of those strategies.

Check with Your Sources

If you've learned that flowers and ties are out, ask Mom and Dad what they'd really like as a gift. If they balk and say, "Oh, I have everything I need," assure them that you're going to give them a gift regardless and that, since you want to get something for Mother's Day or Father's Day that they'll use and enjoy, they should volunteer some ideas. If that doesn't pan out, then start asking questions.

Again, like a reporter, you need to be observant and unafraid to ask questions. So give these queries a whirl: "Are there any books you've been meaning to read that I can buy for you?" or "Did you enjoy a nice bottle of wine recently that you'd like to have in the house?" or "Is there any restaurant nearby where you've wanted to eat? Maybe I can make reservations for us."

Tie in a Hobby

The hobbies or pastimes your mom or dad enjoys can be a springboard to excellent gifts. My mother the bird-watcher is also an avid gardener. So, if I wanted to give her flowers for Mother's Day, I probably wouldn't send a bouquet from the florist (although I'm sure she'd find them pretty). Rather, more appropriate for her would be a flat of annuals that she could plant in her garden. And if I could arrange it, I'd spend Mother's Day with her, digging in the dirt.

Does your dad have a fondness for going to the movies? If so, offer to take him to the latest release on Father's Day and then out to eat at his favorite restaurant. If you don't live nearby, send him a gift certificate to the movies, or a gift card from a local video store so he can enjoy seeing a film as a gift from you.

Offer an Indulgence

If there's one universal truth about parents, it's that they don't often indulge themselves as much as they should. To remedy this situation, circle Mother's Day and Father's Day on your calendar as the perfect time to give them the gift of indulgence. Choose a box of chocolates for either parent if they love chocolates. Or, if you think they'd appreciate and use it, a certificate for an afternoon of pampering at a nearby spa. For a parent who lives alone or has a busy schedule, arrange for a cleaning service to take care of the house or for a catering service to deliver meals so Mom or Dad doesn't have to cook for a few days. All of these gifts say, "Take a well-earned break" and should soothe the body as well as the spirit.

If You've Got Children, Use Them for Inspiration

My husband and I can both attest that as far as our own moms and dads are concerned, anything made by or featuring their grandchildren is a gift worth more than gold. If you've got children and your mind is blocked about what would be a good Mother's Day or Father's Day gift, look to the kids for inspiration. We have a paint-your-own pottery store nearby where kids can create a vase, candy dish, or jewelry box. If I were ever at a loss for a Mother's Day or Father's Day gift, I'd bring my children to this store and set them loose making something for their grandmother or grandfather.

Pictures of your children, always a solid gift for parents, take the cake on Mother's Day or Father's Day. Snap some photos of your children in front of a pretty spring-like background and then place those shots in a frame. If you want to commemorate the occasion, buy a frame that says "Happy Mother's Day" or something like that.

Give What You Enjoy

When in doubt, a good resort is to give something you enjoy. If you've read a book that you think Mom or Dad would find compelling, buy another copy as your gift. Do the same with a CD or a bottle of wine. Enclose a handwritten note that explains why you've chosen the gift—that you recently enjoyed the same thing, and you thought your mom or dad would have a similarly positive reaction. I'm sure they'll receive this gift in the spirit in which it was intended.

*   *   *   *   *

Welcome to the Real World: Graduation

When I graduated from college, my parents got together and bought me a computer. It was the perfect present for me since I had just earned a degree in journalism, and I knew I wanted to pursue freelance writing. The best way for me to do that was to have the latest computer technology at home and not to have to rely on the second-hand computer that got me through college. I used and abused that new computer, and eventually I upgraded to an even better model when I was earning sufficient money as a writer and could afford to do so. I couldn't have launched my professional writing career without that old, now obsolete computer, which is why it's one of my never-to-be-forgotten graduation gifts.

Get Technical

One of the best gifts you can give a graduating high school or college senior is a computer. Many colleges require incoming freshmen to have certain technology at their disposal, so a computer gift helps send a college-bound teen off fully equipped. Likewise, most college graduates heading out into the real world rely on a home computer to surf the Net for jobs or just for E-mailing.

If swinging the entire purchase is too much for you, going in with a couple of friends or family members can make it an affordable group gift. Of course, don't go computer shopping without first checking with the graduate's parents. They may be planning to buy a computer themselves for their son or daughter, rendering your gift redundant. In that event, one of these related options could be the perfect solution:

- Find out the machine's specs and give compatible software, such as an accounting program for keeping track of finances.
- Offer to buy a printer or scanner.
- Buy a half dozen or so printer cartridges and a ream of paper, both pricey parts that will surely come in handy down the road.
- Give a gift certificate to a store where the graduate can get electronics supplies and accessories—whether it's the college's bookstore or a local Staples or Office Depot.

Give a gift certificate to an e-tailer or a bricks-and-mortar store with an online presence, such as Barnes & Noble, so the graduate can inaugurate the computer by doing some online shopping. If you'd like to buy technology without buying a computer, you can always consider getting the graduate a new cell phone, Blackberry or other handheld device that will come in handy in the real world.

Sweep Them Away with Housewares

Both high school and college graduates often find themselves in new quarters—a dormitory or apartment—where their need for housewares instantly increases. For these transplants, a gift of housewares can save them time and money.

A lifesaving gift I received before going off to college—and which I've subsequently given to high school graduates many times over—was a laundry basket filled with dormitory necessities: hangers, toothbrush holder, iron, desktop mirror, a gallon of laundry detergent, and an alarm clock. You can fill up your own basket or tub based on the needs of the recipient. Then, to wrap it up, buy a large roll of cellophane and create the perfect gift basket secured with ribbon or a bow.

For the college graduate, anything that can help furnish a first apartment or home would be welcomed. A set of contemporary cooking pots or baking pans are essentials, as are bed linens or bath towels. If you're unsure what the person wants or likes, you can go with a gift certificate to a home furnishings store so she can do the shopping on her own time.

Dress Them for Success

While I was more than grateful for the computer that my parents gave me for my college graduation, what I could have used as well was some help updating my wardrobe—or at least some guidance on how to dress for job interviews. I still cringe when I think back at what a fashion emergency I was when I was going on those first job interviews. I had no idea what kind of jacket to wear, or that investing in new clothes would not only make me look professional but increase my confidence as well as I interviewed for jobs at magazines. Thus, I think a smart gift for college graduation is a gift certificate from a store with a line of business clothes. Department stores qualify, as do high-end retailers such as Ann Taylor for women, Jos A. Banks for men, and Banana Republic for both genders. The college graduate in question may also benefit from the services of a personal shopper, which could be a considerate add-on to your gift certificate. All-encompassing department stores like Nordstrom do a fabulous job of working one-on-one with their clientele.

❧ The Best Gift I Ever Gave ❧

I had a really close-knit group of friends in college. Right before graduation, I put together a photo album of pictures of us—from freshman to senior years. I added quotes and inside jokes underneath each picture. Then I made five color copies of the book so I could give one to each of my friends. I put a different cover on each album, and then wrote a personal letter to each friend on the last page. That was my graduation gift to all, and even now, years later when we get together, we'll all reminisce while looking at these handmade photo album.

Stacy, New York

❧*The Best Gift I Ever Gave* ☙

The gift that I love to give to graduates is a world globe. I love to travel, and I love to encourage others to do so as well. A globe introduces the concept of the world and is a great way to whet the person's appetite to travel to various places.

Katharine, Quebec

Make It Money

If you can't determine a specific gift to give a graduate, go with greenbacks. A student who'll be entering college can use it to buy books, and the college grad can apply it to car payments, rent, or travel expenses.

Instead of just slipping a check in an envelope, be a little creative with how you package the gift. For example, with a college-bound graduate, find out which school the student will be attending, and then buy a mug or baseball cap with that school's name or insignia, and place the cash gift inside. (Many colleges and universities sell these kinds of items through their website, so if you don't live near to the school the graduate will be attending, you can always shop online for these items.) For a college graduate who will be traveling to a new location to start a job, package your gift with fun items that represents the move—a foldout map of the new city, a used airline ticket envelope, or a movie that's representative of the new town where the graduate is moving or line of work he's about to start. These movies could be *All the President's Men* or *Broadcast News* for the fresh-faced new journalist or *When Harry Met Sally* for someone moving to the Big Apple.

Gift Giving FYI

The Lenox Gift Company, which is best known for its china and porcelain collectibles, recently amassed a history of gift giving. Here's what the company found out about the tradition of Mother's Day and Father's Day:

- The first Mother's Day was observed on May 10, 1908, in Grafton, West Virginia. People gathered at church there to honor a local schoolteacher's deceased mother and, by extension, all the mothers who attended the service. That teacher, Anna Jarvis, eventually lobbied the federal government to declare Mother's Day a national holiday. She got her wish six years later when President

Woodrow Wilson signed a proclamation that the second Sunday in May was to be Mother's Day.

- In honor of Mother's Day each year, Americans purchase 10 million bouquets of flowers and exchange 150 million greeting cards. It seems that taking Mom out for a meal is a popular gift, since more people eat out at restaurants on Mother's Day than on any other day of the year.

- Father's Day also had its simple start at a church service in West Virginia. In 1910, a woman named Sonora Smart Dodd realized that her father had sacrificed much to raise her and her five siblings after her mother had died, and that he, like other fathers, deserved a day of tribute. Dodd began a letter-writing campaign to promote the idea of Father's Day, which she proposed be on her father's birthday, June 5.

- Once Mother's Day was accepted as a holiday, the push was on for Father's Day to be recognized equally. Both Presidents Woodrow Wilson and Calvin Coolidge tried to convince Congress of the need for Father's Day, but it wasn't until 1972 that President Richard Nixon officially declared that the second Sunday in June be nationally recognized as Father's Day.

- Father's Day founder Dodd suggested that the rose be the flower of Father's Day—a white rose to honor a deceased father, and a red rose to honor a living father. While we don't hear much about roses and fathers, the rose is considered the flower of choice for Father's Day.

- Americans buy about 95 million Father's Day cards each year, but only about 16 percent of them take Dad out for a meal that day.

❧ 9 ⇜

WHAT TO DO FOR WEDDINGS

Weddings are perhaps the least complex present-buying situation you'll face in your gift-giving life: the couple registers for gifts, and you use that registry as a printed guide. Or, if you live in an area where giving money is more accepted than giving china, you write out a check, and you're all set. But chances are, the wedding isn't the only time you'll be giving the happy couple a gift. Before anyone walks down the aisle, you'll probably get invitations to engagement parties and at least one bridal shower. Between the betrothal and the ceremony itself, you're going to be doing a lot of shopping.

You already know that I advocate giving repeat gifts—or at least ones that are related—when they've gone over big for birthdays and holidays. However, you may have to make an exception to that rule when it comes to the series of gifts you'll be buying and giving for an engagement party, a bridal shower, and then a wedding. Sure, it might be efficient to purchase three place settings of the couple's china and then give one for each occasion. But if the couple hasn't registered or you live in a place where the gift of money is more accepted than the gift of china, you may find yourself in an awkward position if you come bearing a place setting of china for each of these occasions. To help you along I've devoted this chapter to ideas on some old, new, borrowed, and blue ideas for each of the gift-giving scenarios you're likely to encounter when a friend, colleague, or relative gets ready to tie the knot.

Engagement Gifts

When my husband and I got engaged, I was pleased when people sent me congratulations cards, but I was really touched when we received unexpected engagement gifts. Now, understand that you're not expected to send an engagement gift when someone announces the big news, although it's nice if you can. However, if you are invited to an engagement party (which oftentimes turns into a mini-wedding), it's absolutely expected that you take a gift. If you can't attend the festivities, you should at least send a little something to commemorate the newly announced engagement.

❧The Best Gift I Ever Gave ❧

For my sister, I put together a bridal gift that was a box of household hints, which I'd collected over the years. Each hint was taped to the substance that you would use to solve a household dilemma. For example, to a bottle of vinegar I taped "Pour vinegar over your hands to eliminate onion odors." Years later, she told me that whenever she or her husband was faced with a household quandary, her husband would tell her to look at my box to see if there was an answer there.

Marty, New York

Wedding-Planning Books

One of my favorite engagement gifts was a wedding-planning book from my maid of honor. She gave it to me almost immediately after our announcement, and before I'd had the chance to go to the bookstore myself and start perusing the wedding racks. While I still wound up buying additional guides to match my specific needs, this general how-to on wedding basics was an indispensable tool, and a gift to consider for any newly engaged woman.

One of the reasons I loved that wedding-planning book is that it laid out everything I needed to know to organize myself and to do a better job of lining up the vendors I would have to hire for my wedding—a caterer, a photographer, and more. I recently came across that trusty planner, and I found myself reading all the notes I'd written to myself in the margins about things I wanted at my wedding. It also contained pictures of hats and shoes that I admired and hoped to buy, which I'd clipped from magazines and slipped between the pages. Revisiting that book was like taking the proverbial stroll down memory lane; it jogged memories of my wedding in a way photographs never could, because it allowed me to go inside my head and relive what I was thinking and going through at the time. It also reminded me how much the gift meant to me—and still does.

If you're going to buy a book that's primarily for the bride's use, complement the gift by buying a book for the groom as well. (Full disclosure: I've written eight books on wedding planning, so I've got a vested interest in encouraging you to buy these kinds of books as gifts. Then again, you may find some real value in my books, which I hope you'll consider purchasing as an engagement present.)

One of my recent books for the bride was written in concert with a book for a groom. Mine is *The Complete Guide for the Anxious Bride*. This other book is called *The Complete Guide for the Anxious Groom* and together they'd make the perfect his-and-her engagement gift.

Picture Frames

Another noteworthy engagement gift we received was a pretty pewter frame. First Bill and I put our engagement picture in the frame; then we put our wedding portrait in it. That framed portrait is still prominently displayed in our home. The combination of functionality, versatility, and sentimental attachment makes a picture frame a timeless engagement gift—especially given the amount of photographs the bride and groom are likely to end up with after their wedding.

Gift Giving FYI

While I'm a huge advocate of shopping off the bride and groom's registry list, there are times when shopping from the actual *store* where the couple registered is out of the question. If you don't live near the merchant at which the couple is registered—and that merchant doesn't offer an online or catalog shopping option—then a good place to find an item is the Ross-Simons catalog. This Rhode Island-based cataloger has come through in a pinch for me many times when I wanted a place setting of china for someone but, for whatever reason, the specified store wasn't going to work for me. Ross-Simons was even a lifesaver for guests at my own wedding, when the Lenox china I'd requested was back-ordered from the local department stores. Ross-Simons had it in stock, available for immediate shipping, *and* at a price that was about 20 percent less than what the department stores were charging.

The company is also a reliable source for silver, crystal, jewelry, linens, and other decorative housewares that make terrific housewarming gifts. As a bonus, the catalog has its own gift registry program, which is a wonderful choice when you're getting married and want to give your guests across the country no-hassle access to *your* registry. To receive a Ross-Simons catalog call (800) 458-4545 or visit the online store at ross-simons.com.

Buying off the Registry

If the newly engaged couple is really on the ball, they might already have registered for gifts, which means you have another option for choosing an engagement gift. If this is the case, one of the smaller, more personal items on the registry would be a fine engagement gift to give. Here again, perhaps a picture frame. If the couple has registered for some funky stuff, like margarita glasses or other fun barware, you can buy four or eight of the glasses, and then package them with a recipe guide on making the perfect margarita or martini, along with an accompanying bottle of liquor.

Gifts That Give Stress Relief

As soon as a couple starts putting together a wedding "to do" list, the old blood pressure starts going up. This is the best time for a gift that lets them blow off steam, or at least relax. You'll do both if you treat them to a couple's massage, which many spas today offer. This kind of indulgence lets them savor some downtime together. Or collaborate with a group of friends and pay for a restful weekend away at a country inn. For some serious blowing-off-steam, you could purchase certificates for a set of kickboxing or karate classes to take together, or give them the gift of laughter, which is a great stress reliever, by treating them to a night out at a comedy club. All are terrific twists on the traditional engagement gift.

Bridal Showers

I'm always pleased when a bridal shower has a theme, because it makes getting a gift for the occasion so much easier. If, say, you're invited to a kitchen-themed event, you know to direct your gift-related thoughts to cookware or other culinary items. (Ideally, the couple will have registered, and you can scan the official wish list for everything in the kitchen.) If you go to a lingerie bridal shower, the gift field is equally obvious: something sexy, something slinky, something for the bedroom. But what is the right gift for when you've been invited to a regular old bridal shower—one for which there's no theme, and is perhaps in honor of a bride you don't know well, like your new husband's second cousin's fiancée? Here are some tried-and-true tips for buying great bridal shower gifts.

Consult the Registry

Most shower invitations these days come with information about where the couple has registered. If yours doesn't, find out where the bride is registered by calling the shower hostess or asking the parents, if you know them. Then, your only quandary is how much to spend.

A single place setting of china is usually in most people's price range—that is, if the bride and groom were thoughtful when registering. It drives me crazy when I get a copy of a registry and realize that the bride and groom obviously had no qualms about asking for everything expensive in the store—and no consideration of the fact that different people have different budgets for wedding gifts. For example, not that I was invited to this celebration, but I know for a fact that for Donald Trump's recent wedding, he registered for a silver coffee pot and a silver tea pot, each of which cost $4,000. Who really needs something so extravagant?

When it comes to wedding registries, I always advise couples to register for a wide price range of items. By doing so, you give people the option of going all out and buying you the $500 soup tureen or the $4,000 silver coffee pot, or keeping it simple by getting you a $25 picture frame.

If you're staring at a registry list with only high-priced items on it, you have two choices: one, find other people to go in on the gift with you, which will allow you to buy more and have everyone spend less; or two, buy a non-registry gift—one with a price tag that doesn't send your budget into a nosedive. Again, even though I'm an advocate for buying off of a couple's registry, if you can't afford anything on the registry, I don't want you to go into debt satisfying the bride and the groom's gift-getting needs. This would be the one instance where I would encourage you not to buy from the registry but instead to find an affordable and meaningful gift elsewhere.

❧The Best Gift I Ever Gave ❧

When my best friend and his wife got engaged, they registered for gifts at a cookware store. Ordinarily, I shop off the registry, since I figure people now best what they want and need. However, this was a special friend, and I wanted to make a special effort—particularly since I knew they both had crazy schedules and often ate frozen dinners cooked in the microwave. I decided to give them a gift that would help them appreciate any high-end kitchen gadgets they'd be receiving from their registry: a personal chef, albeit for the short term. Through a local cooking school, I arranged to have a chef come to their home and use their cookware to prepare food and to demonstrate his techniques every step of the way. The idea was to leave them with several fast-but-healthy recipes and some new culinary skills. Needless to say, this gift was a huge hit, and they still remark that it was one of the best gifts they received.

Fawn California

Gift-Giving FAQs

Q. *I have to give a wedding gift to two somewhat "offbeat" people, and I don't think they want a regular wedding gift, I want to give them something, but I don't know where to start. Help!*
A: The first thing you need is to find out if the couple has registered at a store. While you say that this duo is "offbeat," even the most artsy of couples have been known to register their gift preferences, usually to comply with family wishes. So, ask, and you may just receive a solution to your gift-giving dilemma.

What if they *didn't* register? Well, then, you've got some investigating to do. Start asking yourself some questions about this couple, assuming that you know them well. (If you don't, I've got a standard gift to give, but more about that later.) How is their home decorated? What do they like to do in their free time? What are their careers? Answers to these questions can guide you in your gift search. For example, if this couple is very down-to-earth and enjoys outdoorsy activities, a gift certificate to any store than promotes an active lifestyle is probably a safe bet. Retailers such as L.L.Bean, REI, and Eastern Mountain Sports spring to mind. If they like to cook or entertain, you may want to pick something kitchen-related from Williams-Sonoma, Crate & Barrel, or Pottery Barn. (Note: I'm mentioning national stores because of their countrywide access, but that doesn't mean that you can't shop locally. I'm a proponent of supporting local, small businesses, so if you frequent one that may fulfill your gift-giving needs, by all means shop there.)

As for the standard gift I promised to tell you about, here it is: go buy something from Tiffany. Your gift will come packaged in Tiffany's trademark robin's egg blue box and tied with a crisp white ribbon, and it's bound to be a big hit with the recipients. My favorite I-don't-know-you-very-well-but-I-wanted-you-to-have-a-nice-engagement/wedding-gift purchase is Tiffany's crystal ice bucket (about $80, last time I looked). I got one when I got married, and it's a cherished item that I use whenever I entertain. My guess is others will find it to be a wonderful gift as well.

Q: *I know it's important to buy a wedding gift off the couple's registry, but I'm a procrastinator. As a consequence, by the time I get around to finding a copy of the list, everything has already been purchased. What can I do?*
A: First, your friends or relatives who've been getting married must know some very generous people. In all my years in this business, I've yet to come across a gift wish list on which everything is accounted for. What is more likely, for me and probably for lots of other people, is that all the gifts in your *price range* have been spoken for, so you're left with getting either the $12.99 corkscrew or the $500 bone china serving platter. So, what do you do? Get creative.

Let's take that $12.99 corkscrew for openers (no pun intended). On its own, it seems like an awfully measly present, but if you add other wine-related gifts to it, it'll be awesome. If I were facing a registry list with only the corkscrew left on it, I'd buy the corkscrew, but then I'd invest in a case of good wine (red or white, depending on the couple's preference), then four amazing wine glasses, and maybe a wine rack. Or how about this? If the couple lives in a region known for its wine, buy the corkscrew, but then put it in a box along with a reservation for a weekend in the nearby wine country. Eastern Long Island in New York and California's Napa and Sonoma Valleys are all areas known for their wine making. Finally, certain wineries across the country will create personalized labels on bottles of wine so that you can, in essence, create your own vintage. Along with the corkscrew, give them a case of wine in which every bottle has a label that wishes them congratulations or bears their names and their wedding date. (Three vineyards that do custom labeling—Chaddsford Winery, New Hope Winery, and Windsor Vineyards—are described in Chapter 7.)

Another way to get creative is to use the already-filled registry list as a guide to other gifts that will coordinate with the stuff on the registry. The fact that the items have already been purchased doesn't mean you can't look at them. For example, go see firsthand the kinds and colors of linens that the bride and groom registered for. If, for example, the couple is going for a Western theme, with denim slipcovers and bandana print pillows, buy them some Western-inspired housewares, such as coasters in the shape of a sheriff's star or hurricane lamps that look as if they'd be at home on the range. Or if the registry indicates a more retro look, log on to eBay or visit a local antiques fair for cool glasses, serving bowls, or vases that will go with those items.

Size Up Housewares

When you're not working from a registry list, you're still safe with a housewares gift: a cheery pottery serving bowl, a pair of candlesticks and a box of decorative candles—you get the picture. Everyone has a use for gifts such as these, regardless of how often the couple entertains. For example, in my home, we tend to keep the breakables on the top shelves of our entertainment center because of our two active children. But look there and you'll find all of the glassware, serving bowls, and candlesticks we've received over the years. They add a decorative flair to the furnishings, and when we entertain, we put them to good use.

There are plenty of these types of gifts in any one of the national housewares retailers—Bed, Bath & Beyond, Pier One, or Crate & Barrel, to name a few. I also like to shop in unique boutiques, like the one in my town that carries Fiestaware pieces and one-of-a-kind pottery. My favorite gift to buy there is supersize coffee mugs, like the ones used at Central Perk on "Friends." I drink these up because they're conducive for someone who drinks coffee as well as someone who doesn't—they can hold hot chocolate, tea, pencils, or can simply decorate a shelf.

TLC for the Bride-to-Be

When in doubt, gifts that pamper are always well received. If there's anything that's true about a busy bride-to-be, it's that she doesn't slow down often enough to give herself some tender loving care. Thus, when she receives a gift that's all about pampering, she will immediately think, "Hey, when can I use this?" Two of my favorite pampering gifts over the years have been bath salts, which reintroduced me to the glory of soaking in a tub, and gift certificates for spa treatments.

For a package of gifts in this realm, look into the clever pampering "kits" on the market these days. They might come packaged in something cute, like a paint can, and include everything needed to turn an ordinary bathroom into a luxurious at-home spa: bath salts, body scrub, yummy scented lotions, a CD of soothing music, and an aromatherapy candle.

If you'd like to shower the bride with pampering time away from home, find out where she goes to get her hair cut or her favorite nail salon, and buy her a gift certificate for a manicure, scalp massage, or similar service. Or buy her a certificate for use at a place that you like and trust—that is, if you live near one another, of course. If you don't live close by or know much about pampering services, you can check out one of these spa clearinghouses that will help you pinpoint a reputable spa in the bride's hometown and purchase a gift certificate for a specific service. They are: SpaFinders at (800) ALL-SPAS (255-7727) or www.spafinders.com; or SpaWish at (888) SPA-WISH (772-9474) or www.spawish.com.

❧The Best Gift I Ever Got ❧

At my bridal shower, I received a pair of hand-knit Christmas stockings. On the front of one was my name, and on the front of the other was my husband's name. On the back of each was our wedding date. It was such a thoughtful gift, and we continue to use these stockings every year at Christmas.

Laura, New York

Wedding Gifts—and Customs to Consider

Having grown up on the East Coast—New York, to be precise—I was raised to believe that when you go to a wedding, you hand the bride and groom a check, and you call it a day. This is how I routinely congratulated friends and family when they tied the knot, and no one ever gave it a second thought. Then, shortly after my husband Bill and had our own wedding (in New York, by the way, where most of the guests gave us the gift of cash), we moved to Michigan so Bill could attend graduate school. While there, we made friends with many couples and were invited to several weddings. It was just before the first of those weddings that I happened to be discussing gifts with another woman, who was born and raised in the Midwest. I mentioned that I was planning on giving the happy couple a check. Her face froze, her jaw dropped, and she gasped, "You're going to do what?"

"Give them money," I repeated.

"Why don't you just slap them in the face instead?" she suggested.

After my own jaw dropped, I asked her to explain. I suddenly felt like a foreigner in a foreign land.

After a quick lesson on local customs, I learned that while money was an acceptable—if not the preferred—gift for brides and grooms in the Northeast, in the Midwest that was not so. When you arrive at a Midwest wedding, you bring a box, not an envelope. Giving a gift of money is seen as a slap in the face, and only the most insensitive guests just write a check (probably how East Coast folks like myself got a bad rap in this section of the country). I also learned that according to local etiquette, your first course of action is to buy the bride and groom a gift off their registry. If the couple is not registered, then your second option is to buy something nice from the china or housewares section of the local department store. Your third option—well, there really isn't one, since money is out of the question, so you should make option one or two work.

At that time, I was just starting my career as a wedding writer and gift-giving adviser. The last thing I wanted to do was commit a social faux pas at my first Midwest wedding so I adjusted my gift giving accordingly.

When I was ready to shop, I headed to my local department store, found the couple's registry, and bought a handful of the silver flatware they'd requested. For the next wedding, I went back to that same department store, got the registry, and secured six pieces of the crystal they'd designated. The wedding after that, I went for two place settings of their china off that department store registry list. The newlyweds happily accepted each of those gifts, and I came away with a better appreciation of the gift registry's role in facilitating the gift-giving process.

Probably the most important lesson I learned from my Midwest experience was this: You must know the customs and etiquette that apply in the area where you'll be attending a wedding, and keep them in mind when selecting a gift. If you're a New Yorker flying to Texas for a wedding, do your homework prior to settling on a gift. Find out if money is OK to give at a Texas wedding before you hand over the check. If it's not, get yourself a copy of the couple's registry so you can make a socially correct choice. After attending weddings nationwide, I've concluded that a gift from the registry is more widely accepted than a gift of money. So, if there's a shadow of a doubt (even in the Northeast), you can give a gift with confidence if you stick with the couple's registry.

Finally, even if you don't attend a wedding to which you're invited, you should still send a gift. Etiquette rules state that you have up to a year after the wedding to do so, but I think it's best to do it right away—almost as soon as you receive the invitation and send back your regrets. Not only will you have done the bride and groom right, but also by buying the gift now and not putting it off, you won't run the risk of actually forgetting to buy them a gift later on.

❧ The Best Gift I Ever Got ❧

For our wedding, my husband's two sisters gave us an antique writing table, which I still have today. It's a unique piece, and I still look at it and remember sitting there and writing all of my thank-you notes

Kathleen, Pennsylvania

❧ The Best Gift I Ever Gave ❧

I like to give gifts with a theme for bridal showers, and my favorite of late is this one: a pizza stone, plus other pizza-making tools, topped off with a cookbook filled with unique ways to make a pizza pie.

Mandy, California

❧ 10 ❦

BONUS GIFT-GIVING SECTION

There are plenty of gift-giving occasions where you'd like your present to go above and beyond a gift you might find shopping at the mall. Maybe you'd like to do your shopping in cyberspace, because you found this really great website offering fabulous gifts you know your recipient would love. Or perhaps you're intent on gifts that benefit a good cause, because you know that the recipient will appreciate the extra effort you've made to give a gift that gives back. Other times, you may want to send a gift that represents your hometown or your state mammal, because going for the local touch will make your gift that more special. And don't forget party favors for your guests—these are a good idea when you're hosting a celebration where favors make sense, such as a child's birthday party or a baby shower. Finally, when you're on the receiving end of a gift, you should always write a thank-you note. Unfortunately, thank-you notes have become a lost art but they don't have to be if you know how to write a heartfelt thank you in no time.

This final chapter ties up these loose ends about gift giving in five sections:

- Being a Smart Internet Shopper
- Gifts for Your Guests
- Gifts That Benefit a Good Cause
- Gifts of Place
- How to Write Thank-You Notes

Being a Smart Internet Shopper

I've been an avid online shopper since 1998. I've never had a problem with goods not being delivered or my credit card number being lifted. Then again, I tend to stick to the more mainstream sites at which I'm confident I'll be treated well. If that's your preferred method of shopping online, you may want to hear about my friend Jamie who learned her lesson about how to shop (or bid) smartly online.

A Rude Introduction to OnLine Auctions

Jamie is a big fan of Eddie Izzard, the cross-dressing British comedian who has had several specials on HBO. A few years ago, she was planning a dinner party and wanted to show a video of Izzard's antics as the evening's entertainment. The only problem: at that time, Izzard's performances weren't readily available in the United States. So, Jamie, who shops online at least once a month, visited Amazon.com's auctions in search of an Izzard tape. She found two, listed by a seller named "Mrs. Badcrumble." After bidding $71 and winning, Jamie eagerly sent a check to the seller, who cashed it in early November. By Christmas, Jamie still had no Eddie Izzard videos. (I think the seller's name should have been her first clue.)

Unfortunately, Jamie's tale of E-woe is common. You might think that the greatest potential for getting ripped off online comes from a hacker getting your credit card number from an e-tailer's website, but according to the National Consumers League, a nonprofit organization dedicated to consumer issues, online auctions have ranked number one for online fraud since 1997. And your rip-off risk of shopping online doesn't correspond to fraud or misuse of credit card information. The real risk lies in paying with a check or money order, as Jamie can tell you.

Credit Cards Are a Must

As a matter of fact, the best way to ensure that you won't get fleeced online is to pay by credit card. If you have a problem with your transaction, the credit card company will go to bat for you to resolve it. If Jamie had paid with good old plastic, she might have been able to wield the muscle of MasterCard in getting Mrs. Badcrumble to cough up the goods. Moreover, while she was disputing the charge, she wouldn't have had to pay it. But once Mrs. Badcrumble cashed her check, her money was gone. And because Jamie hadn't checked or couldn't check on Mrs. Badcrumble's background (a la the Feedback scores you'll find on eBay), she had no way of knowing what a bad cookie Mrs. Badcrumble really was.

Nevertheless, online security is a difficult issue, and many shoppers are reluctant to use credit cards for electronic purchases. (A good alternative is paying with PayPal, a third-party escrow company, if you will, that is owned by eBay and offers a secure way of paying for online purchases.) The best course is to err on the side of caution. Even though, statistically, most Web fraud does not involve credit cards, you can't be too careful when shopping online. And given that research shows that not every American currently shops online, a little tutorial on what to look for in the websites where you're considered shopping couldn't hurt. Here are some must-have features to seek out:

A Secure Server

A secure server encrypts the data on the site to prevent inquiring minds and fraudulent fingertips from gaining access to your personal information, including your credit card number. How can you tell if an online merchant uses a secure server? First, read the site's security statement, which is usually located at the bottom of the home page. Second, look for two important pieces of information on the site itself: the plural URL and the lock.

The Plural URL. When you enter a site's secure server, look for a change in the URL (short for "uniform resource locator"—the website's address): the prefix of "http" will become "https."

Lock It Up. At the same time that the URL changes, you'll notice that the icon of a closed padlock or a key (depending on your browser) appears on the periphery of the page. This is another way for the site and your browser to let you know that you've entered a secure site. (Your browser may also be programmed to have a pop-up window appear when you've entered a secure site. This is yet another positive indication that you're entering a secure portion of a website.)

If you don't see either of those "locked" icons or a change in the URL when you get to a page that asks you for private information, or your browser doesn't tell you that you're on a secure site, by providing a pop up window that says just that, you've got to log out of that site and go shopping elsewhere. You can't be sure the site has a secure server, and you shouldn't take that risk.

A Strict Privacy Policy

Keeping your credit card information secure shouldn't be your only concern when shopping online. Also make sure that any online retailer with which you want to do business has a privacy policy in place (look for the statement on the home page). The site should promise that it won't peddle your personal information, including E-mail address, to other online merchants. (This practice could lead to an E-mailbox filled with spam, or unwanted mail.)

Online Shopping FYI

Even with a stellar privacy policy, there are times when a website or its affiliate companies may want to send you unsolicited email. If you don't want this kind of email clog-
ging up your mailbox, I would suggest setting up an alternative email address that you
use exclusively for your online shopping pursuits. You can get a free email address from
places like Yahoo.com and Hotmail.com, or if your email provider lets you register multiple email monikers under the same account, you could set up a shopping-exclusive
address. Once you do this, always use this address when you register to shop at a website.
Not only will this cut down on spam in your mailbox but also it will allow you to keep
all of your shopping-related emails in one place.

A Good Track Record Is a Must

It's also wise to do some research and shop only on sites that have treated others
well. For commentary on how various e-tailers have performed, go to
BizRate.com, an independent rating company that surveys online buyers at the
time they make a purchase—and again a week later when, ideally, the merchandise should have arrived. One site where I shop that uses BizRate.com is
Staples.com (for office supplies). Whenever I complete an order, a BizRate window pops up and asks me to rate my shopping experience. This information is
used to grade online merchants and award them anywhere from one to five gold
stars. Currently, BizRate gives the lowdown on about three thousand sites.

If you're shopping on auction sites, you must check a seller's feedback rating
before making purchases. For example, on eBay, you want to look for a seller with
a Feedback rating of 100 percent or near to that. Also, make sure that you read
the comments from previous buyers to make sure that the seller offers good com-
munication, fast shipping and all of the positive traits you prize in any online
company, such as a mail-order catalog.

A less technical way of sizing up an e-tailer is to ask people you know who
shop online where they go to buy their stuff and how they've been treated there.

Place Your Trust in Reputable Websites

You only want to deal with an auction site or e-tailers that will stand behind its
services, as Amazon.com did with Jamie. She filed a complaint about "Mrs.
Badcrumble," and shortly after Christmas, Amazon.com refunded her $71.
While that made Jamie feel very good about Amazon.com—where she has con-

tinued to do her online shopping and bidding—it still left her wanting those Eddie Izzard videotapes. I think she eventually found them on good old eBay!

* * * * *

Gifts for Your Guests

Along with the occasions when we thank our hosts with a gift, there are times when we, as the hosts, don't want to send our guests off empty-handed. People who attend your child's birthday party, your wedding, your baby shower, or a dinner party are all candidates for such recognition. When you want to make your guests feel special, use some of the ideas in this section for goodie bags, favors, and mementos.

Children's Birthday Parties

When my daughter Jane turned four, I created a party favor that held appeal for children and parents alike, because it was both practical and fun. I started with a stack of brightly colored twenty-eight-ounce plastic tumblers. Using sparkly paint pens, I wrote each child's name on one of the cups. Then, inside I put some candy, a bottle of bubbles, and either plastic jewelry and hair accessories for girls or drinking straws featuring *Star Wars* characters for boys. I wrapped the entire ensemble in clear cellophane and tied it with ribbon so that it looked a little like a festive pineapple. The end result? A professional-looking favor that cost just a few dollars each to make.

Other unusual ideas for birthday party favors include:

- Small tubs of Play-Doh and plastic cookie cutters
- Tie-dyed T-shirts that commemorate your child's birthday celebration
- Lunchbox-type containers packed with crayons and a coloring book, rubber stamps, stickers, or temporary tattoos

If the group is older, instead of toys, give each guest a gift bag with a store gift card inside. I usually recommend cards in a $10 denomination from the kinds of stores favored by preteens and teens—booksellers, video stores, electronics retailers, or mass merchants where there's something for everyone. Or give them a gift certificate to the local movie theater chain—basically, something they can enjoy using in their free time and with their friends.

Wedding Receptions

Where I grew up, candy-covered almonds wrapped in tulle were the de rigueur wedding favor. Sure, guests eat them up, but when you want to buck tradition, consider the following suggestions:

- Freshly potted seasonal flowers or plants, such as a poinsettia for a December wedding or a pot of petunias for a spring wedding
- Votive candles
- A small box of chocolates or a cluster of Hershey's Kisses wrapped in pretty fabric or enclosed in foil gift bags
- Small picture frames, which can double as holders for seat assignment cards
- Personalized bottles of wine—buy by the case from a winery that will let you custom-design a label with your name and wedding date, and then offer these as a toast to your guests
- Souvenirs of the place where you were married—for example, if you hold a destination wedding in Hawaii, give each guest a fresh-flower lei. For a weekend wedding in Vermont, present them with fancy bottles of maple syrup in a brown bag decorated with pine-cone-shape stamps in silver and gold.
- Instead of sending your gets home with tscotckes, why not make a donation to a charity instead? For ideas on how you can pull this off, I would recommend visiting two great websites: idofoundation.org and married-forgood.com.

Baby Showers

It's always fun to throw an expectant mom a baby shower. You get to make a fuss over the roundness of her belly and laugh as everyone shares crazy cravings stories. Not only do you want to celebrate the upcoming arrival, you also want the women who attend to carry away a little treasure as well. Here are two suggestions for fun favors:

- *Notepaper.* You can buy off the rack in a card store, or opt for more distinguished stock—maybe pastel-colored cards that a local artist created. For a note of elegance, seek out cards that feature pressed flowers or prints from a local museum.
- *Anything pampering.* Give bath salts, hand creams, or sweet-smelling soaps, and attach a note that says you want your guests to "baby" them-

selves with this gift. Good sources of these kinds of pampering products are stores that sell Caswell-Massey and Lady Primrose brands, as well as spas and beauty salons. Mall stores like Bath & Body Works also carry pampering products that would make great baby shower favors.

Dinner Parties

I recently attended a dinner party given by a woman who is known around town for her out-of-this-world cookies. Whenever our children's school needs someone to bake cookies for class parties or fund-raisers, this woman steps up to the table—and leaves us hungry for more. She knows that everyone goes bonkers over her baked goods, and she likes to keep her fans salivating by not revealing the recipe. However, as dinner guests in her home, we were given a special treat to take home: a ball of refrigerated cookie dough, made from her coveted recipe, wrapped in red cellophane and tied with a white bow, from which a cookie cutter hung. While she didn't come clean on exactly how she makes her wonderful cookies, she did send us off with a sample of the batter so we could experience them fresh from the oven. I made that batch the next day with my daughters, and we were in heaven.

If you've earned a reputation for excelling at making something—cookies, a vegetable appetizer, fruit jam—send your dinner party guests home with individual samples of your culinary creation.

Or you can stick with more traditional favors, such as:

- Delicate candles, such as votives or ones that float
- Small, ornate picture frames
- Copies of that evening's menu printed on parchment, rolled into a scroll, and tied with a raffia ribbon; you can even personally inscribe each menu and convey your heartfelt thanks that the person joined you for dinner
- A wrapped package of chocolates or mints

For dinner parties where children are welcomed, have pint-size favors on hand as well, such as Matchbox cars or colored pencils. For a New Year's Eve party we hosted, my daughters decorated brown paper lunch bags and filled them with candy, toys, and noisemakers. We gave them out to all the children who attended. When you remember your smallest guests with a little gift, you'll have happy children *and* parents.

*   *   *   *   *

Gifts That Benefit a Good Cause

Whenever possible, I like to send someone a gift that benefits a good cause. One avenue is buying items from local nonprofit or charitable organizations to help with their fund-raising. For example, this past year some of our family members received holiday decorations that students at my daughter's elementary school had made. The decorations looked professional, and the revenue helped support the school. On other occasions I might select an item that has been earmarked to support a specific cause, such as the pink candle that Avon was selling last year—part of the proceeds went to help fund breast cancer research.

There are hundreds, if not thousands, of other ways to buy gifts with redeeming value. Instead of listing them all here, I've highlighted a few stellar ones to consider the next time you want to buy a do-good gift. (If you want a thorough resource to gifts that benefit a good cause, you can always look on your favorite search engine using the phrase "gifts that benefit a good cause.")

Berea College Crafts

You may remember this institution from Chapter 3. Berea College is a small, liberal-arts school in Berea, Kentucky, that has had a tuition-free policy since its founding in 1855. One of the ways the college supports itself and is able to offer free education to some 1,500 students is through its crafts program, in which students are asked to participate. This program offers apprenticeship opportunities for students to learn iron smithing and woodworking, among other skills. The decorative items they create—from blown glass to wind chimes—are unique, professionally constructed, gorgeous, and not terribly expensive. You can scroll through an extensive list of the items for sale on the college's website at berea.com.

Museum Stores

I love visiting museums, but I'm even more of a connoisseur of their museum stores. I always find unique items, and I know my purchase helps support the facility and its collections. Many museum stores now sell their wares online, so if you can't get to your favorite museum to buy a gift, at least you can get something off of its website.

Heifer Project International

The mission of this charitable organization harks back to the saying "Give a man a fish, and he eats for a day; teach a man to fish, and he eats for a lifetime." A donation to Heifer Project International (HPI), made in the gift recipient's name, ensures the delivery of livestock of various species to a poor family in a poverty-stricken area of the world. You can buy a gift of bees for a family in Ghana for $30, or give a South American family a llama for $150. Since 1944, HPI has helped more than four million families in 118 countries become self-reliant by providing them with farm animals—and training about how to use them to support a family. For a catalog call (800) 422-0474 or go to heifer.org on the Web.

*   *   *   *   *

Gifts of Place

Sometimes the best gift to give someone, regardless of the occasion, is what I call a "gift of place"—an item that perfectly represents a city or state or are the actual items that a place is known for, such as Philadelphia and cheese steaks or Washington and monuments.. These gifts let you memorialize the place where you live, a place where the gift recipient once lived, or a place to which you've traveled.

When we lived in Michigan, our gift of choice on most holidays was anything that featured the maize and blue of the University of Michigan, where my husband was attending graduate school. Whenever we traveled to northern Michigan, famed locally for its annual cherry festival, we'd return home with cherry-related products to give as gifts. Other times, we might give a gift representative of the automobile industry, a cornerstone of Michigan's economy.

If your gift giving is all over the map, consult the following state-by-state guide for items that best embody the places you—or the gift recipient—hold dear and consider these suggested gift ideas.

Alabama

A lot of foods originate in Alabama, including pecans (the state's official nut), Gulf Coast seafood, and muscadine grapes, an especially hearty grape variety that thrives in the southeastern United States. Look for jellies, juices, and wine made from these grapes for a luscious Alabama gift.

Alaska

Since Alaska is well known for its native people, a gift of indigenous arts and crafts is a top choice. Additional items to look for include decorative items made from scrimshaw or anything representing Eskimo culture, such as an ulu knife (pronounced "oo-loo"), which has a hatchet-like blade with a handle attached to the top. This knife's origins date back more than five thousand years, and even in these modern times, it is still considered to be one of the best cutting tools in native Alaskan households.

Arizona

Arizona is graced with one of the world's natural wonders—the Grand Canyon—and a gift that shows its majestic beauty, such as a photograph or painting, would be an excellent choice. The fabled Route 66 also runs through the Grand Canyon State, so keep your eyes peeled for items representing road travel. Also be on the lookout for anything with the saguaro cactus on it, which happens to be the namesake of one of Arizona's national parks.

Arkansas

The mascot of the University of Arkansas is the Razorback, so a gift emblazoned with this wild pig should make an Arkansas fan go hog wild. With the Ozark National Forest near the northwest corner of the state, you'd also want to give an Ozark-crafted item. Whatever you do, pass up the temptation to give any Bill Clinton gag gifts.

California

Several major icons beckon in the Golden State—the Golden Gate Bridge, Yosemite National Park, Hollywood, and the mighty redwood trees—and gifts featuring them should be readily available. In addition, California's renowned wine country, encompassing the Napa and Sonoma Valleys, naturally suggests the gift of spirits. Souvenirs from the state's popular sports attractions are also good picks; these range from Rose Bowl paraphernalia to gear from the California Angels, Oakland A's, or Los Angeles Dodgers.

Colorado

Colorado has more mountains of high elevation than any other state in the country. No wonder there's a profile of a mountain range on the Rocky Mountain
State's license plate. That should put gifts related to the mountains or the skiing
areas of Aspen, Breckenridge, or Boulder high on your list. On a more individual level, even though Colorado is landlocked, Denver was the home of the
Unsinkable Molly Brown, a much-storied Titanic survivor (actress Kathy Bates
portrayed her in the 1997 film *Titanic*). There's a museum in Denver where
you're sure to find nifty Molly Brown memorabilia. Also look for jewelry made
with aquamarine, the state's gemstone.

Connecticut

Connecticut's Mystic Seaport and its magnificent ships are sure to inspire a nautical gift that's right on course. You may be surprised to learn that "Yankee
Doodle" is Connecticut's state song, so a musical gift might be a music box or a
novelty item playing this ditty. Finally, the robin, sperm whale, and praying man-
tis are all official "wildlife" of the Constitution State, giving you an eclectic family of gift possibilities.

Delaware

As with many other East Coast states, Delaware's beaches draw thousands of
tourists every year, so gifts of hand-painted buoys, lighthouse replicas, or anything
with a nautical theme are sure to get a wave of approval. Barring those, the ladybug
is the state insect, so anything incorporating this cute little bug would make a
whimsical remembrance. If you want something historical and related to business,
buy something made from nylon, since Dupont first made this fabric in Delaware.

District of Columbia

Anywhere you turn in our nation's capital, you're a stone's throw from landmarks
and museums, all of which are excellent sources for gifts, souvenirs, and memorabilia—such as models of the White House or the Washington Monument.

Florida

One of the most wholesome gifts from the Sunshine State is one of its principal
crops: oranges. Beyond citrus fruit there's Disney World, Universal Studios, and

Sea World for kitschy or kid-related gifts. Something with an alligator theme, or, for the sports buff, Gatorade, which was developed at the University of Florida, are fun Florida gifts as well. Local artists in the Florida Keys or Miami can be a source of seascape-inspired art, or you can acquire compositions of a different kind—Tom Petty music or Dave Barry books. Both masters of their crafts are from Florida.

Georgia

They don't call Georgia the Peach State because of its shape: peaches are one of its top crops, along with peanuts, and both are popular food gifts. Want something with a longer shelf life? With the duo of Coca-Cola and CNN based here, you've also got your pick of products featuring the logos of these two business behemoths. *Gone with the Wind* was set in Atlanta, and fanciers of Southern culture go crazy for anything having to do with this timeless classic. Finally, I'm sure you can find some leftover Olympic memorabilia from the 1996 Atlanta games on eBay.

Hawaii

Gifts from Hawaii to keep an eye out for include: anything with a picture of a pineapple on it or food with a pineapple flavor; macadamia nuts; locally grown Kona coffee; a hand-crafted ukulele; a grass skirt; an authentic flower lei; or one of those fabulously gaudy Hawaiian shirts.

Idaho

There are three things for which Idaho is best known—and they are ideal resources for gifts from this state: potatoes (Idaho supplies nearly two-thirds of all potatoes in the United States); pine trees (the state has more white pines than any other state); and silver.

Illinois

As the Land of Lincoln, Illinois boasts two Lincoln landmarks: his home in Springfield, which is now a National Historic Site, and his burial place, also in Springfield. Not surprisingly, Springfield, the most visited place in the state, is the spot to find Lincoln memorabilia. Of course, Illinois is also home to the Windy City, Chicago, where options range from gifts from the myriad shops along the Magnificent Mile to items depicting Chicago landmarks to souvenirs embellished with the various sports teams' logos. In addition, there's local music (Chicago blues) and Wrigley's gum (the company is headquartered in Chicago).

Indiana

Talk about your culture clashes. You can give gifts from Indiana that run the gamut from Mennonite crafts and furniture to mementos from the Indianapolis Motor Speedway. Residents of the Hoosier State are rabid sports fans (think of the movie *Hoosiers),* so anything done up in the red and white of Indiana University scores big. Finally, if you're can't resist a gag gift, remember that David Letterman is a native son—take his offbeat humor as your inspiration.

Iowa

Corn is big business here in the Hawkeye State, and gift buyers have plenty of related merchandise to capture the Iowa experience. For snack lovers, you have giant vats of popcorn. For nap lovers, there are even shops that sell corn pillows! Each year, the Iowa State Fair is a big deal and is wide open for buying presents as well.

Kansas

The official symbols of Kansas include sunflowers, bison, and wheat, and the state song is "Home on the Range." Movie buffs will always think of this territory as the setting for *The Wizard of Oz.* "I've a feeling we're not in Kansas anymore," Dorothy mused to Toto in the film; so memorabilia of both the book and the film should blow them away.

Kentucky

One of the best-known, locally made products from Kentucky is the Louisville Slugger, and the factory in Louisville (natch) is open for tours. Next door you'll find an excellent museum on baseball history. Both are home-run sources for gifts. In addition, all horse-racing eyes turn to the Bluegrass State each year for the Kentucky Derby, a source of gift inspiration for horse lovers everywhere.

Louisiana

A gift of beads or anything else representing Mardi Gras in New Orleans will make someone's day. For something a bit spicier, take advantage of the state's rich

Cajun heritage: give 'em a gumbo-making kit (a big pot, spices, and a Louisiana-inspired cookbook) or a bottle of Tabasco (residents' favorite condiment). Also among the possibilities are CDs of Dixieland jazz or the Neville Brothers, or coffee or beignet mix from Café du Monde in New Orleans.

Maine

If you want to make someone who lives (or used to live) in Maine happy, send them lobsters. If you were hoping for something more subtle than a red-shelled crustacean, sail over—anytime—to the venerable retail institution L.L.Bean in Freeport, which is known worldwide for staying open twenty-four hours a day. Give the Maine lover on your list anything featuring a moose, chickadee, or Maine coon cat—all official state animals—and you'll make these Yankees proud. Author Stephen King is a prominent resident and is also an avid supporter of reading and the arts in the Pine Tree State. Choose from among his many titles for a gift that will send chills down the reader's (and gift recipient's) spine.

Maryland

Crabs or anything else in a seafood vein—Chesapeake clam sauce, for example—are good gifts. Or, cast your net over the art inspired by the seascapes on Maryland's eastern shore. Big-city Baltimore has an outstanding aquarium, and don't forget Camden Yards, home of baseball's Baltimore Orioles. You'll find sporting gifts for kids and kids at heart at both places.

Massachusetts

For a small New England state, Massachusetts gives you plenty of gift options—from artist colonies in the western part of the state (the Norman Rockwell museum is here) to fishing communities along the Bay State's two capes, Cape Cod and Cape Ann. There's also the Boston area, which is rich in Colonial memorabilia for the history buffs on your list as well as home to the perennial underdogs, the Boston Red Sox (who, as you know, finally won a World Series in 2004). With its concentration of colleges and universities, Massachusetts is also a mecca for getting collegiate memorabilia and attire: there's Harvard University, MIT, Boston University, Wellesley College, Smith College, Williams College, and Boston College, just to name a few. Walden Pond can inspire a thoughtful gift for literary souls, and for mouth-watering choices there are Boston baked beans and anything with cranberries, a Massachusetts crop, in it.

Michigan

You can't go wrong if you send something featuring the green and white of Michigan State's Spartans or the maize and blue of the University of Michigan's Wolverines. Just make sure to check where your gift recipients' allegiances lie. Sending something green to a Wolverines fan or something blue and gold to a Spartans fan may be grounds for dissolving a friendship. If you want to play it safe, Michigan has the most coastline of any state except for Alaska, so you can comb the shores for items related to water sports or fishing. For music buffs and automobile enthusiasts, there are always goods about Motown or the car industry.

Minnesota

Here in the home of the Mall of America, the country's largest shopping mall, you shouldn't have a problem buying a gift. Garrison Keillor of "A Prairie Home Companion" is based here as well, and you can please radio and music devotees with his works. Gastronomically speaking, Minnesota has two official foods: the blueberry muffin and the morel mushroom.

Mississippi

The magnolia is Mississippi's official flower and tree, and it's a beloved symbol here as is anything having to do with an antebellum theme. In the edibles category, a box of pecan turtles will win the day. (Don't worry: they're chocolates shaped like turtles, not chocolate-dipped turtles.) Or choose a work by or about one of the state's native sons: Elvis Presley (hometown: Tupelo), William Faulkner (hometown: New Albany), or Tennessee Williams (hometown: Columbus). For those who like cutting-edge music, you've got the up-and-coming band North Mississippi All-Stars.

Missouri

The Show-Me State is the place that inspired Samuel Clemens, a.k.a. Mark Twain, what with the Mississippi River and all. Today, besides the landmark St. Louis Arch, many people identify Missouri with Branson, arguably the state's entertainment capital—and a close second to Nashville, Tennessee, as a lightning rod for country music-inspired performers. Missouri is also home to

Anheuser-Busch and the St. Louis Cardinals, both of which could be the source of gift-giving inspiration.

Montana

Thanks to the film *A River Runs Through It*, Montana evokes images of fly-fishing for many folks. And anglers will thank you for your gift of fly-fishing gear or other items related to the sport. Another hook is anything having to do with the vast openness of the state, which is why it's called Big Sky Country. While Helena is the state's official capital, Missoula is probably Montana's cultural and shopping capital and is home to the state's arboretum—a great source of botanical bounty.

Nebraska

Nebraska is where much of the Old West history was made—from Lewis and Clark to the Pony Express. As in Iowa, there's nothing like corn for a locally grown or made gift, such as popcorn or corn on the cob. Omaha Steaks is also based in the Cornhusker State. Here's one for the trivia books and inspiration for a cool kitschy gift: Kool-Aid was created in Hastings, Nebraska, in the 1920s and is the state's official soft drink. You can serve up some of this refreshment for a sweet treat.

Nevada

Take a gamble on Las Vegas-themed gifts (think lounge acts like Wayne Newton and Liberace) or items made of locally mined gemstones or metals, including opal, turquoise, and silver. Nevada residents are sweet on Ethel M chocolate, whose factory you can tour in Henderson and pick up sweets for all. (By the way, the M in Ethel M stands for the Mars Company, maker of M&Ms candy.) Speaking of Mars, Nevada is also home to the infamous Area 51, a hotbed for alleged alien activities and UFO sightings. Pick up a souvenir featuring little green men for anyone you know who is an *X-Files* fan and believes "the truth is out there."

New Hampshire

New Hampshire is best known for its White Mountains, part of the Appalachian Trail and crowned by Mount Washington. Many cars in the Northeast display bumper stickers bragging that the vehicle climbed Mount Washington, and these insignia make great kitschy gifts. You can't go wrong with a sample of the locally produced maple syrup or maple candies; for waistline watchers, beeswax candles are another New Hampshire hallmark. And you'll find fantastic outlet shopping in North Conway, where you should be able to find many New Hampshire-inspired gifts.

New Jersey

Most folks from New Jersey love the Garden State's native musical son, Bruce Springsteen, so anything by him will be a hit. For collectors, steer toward memorabilia of Atlantic City—the heyday of casinos, or the Miss America pageant—or anything having to do with Thomas Edison, who did his inventing in New Jersey. A sweet gift is some saltwater taffy, which was first made in New Jersey years ago. If you're going for a gag, get anything that represents the states two major (and much maligned) highways: the Garden State Parkway and the New Jersey Turnpike.

New Mexico

Like its neighbor Arizona, New Mexico is one of the states that Route 66 crosses, which is your guide for a number of possible gifts. Old gas station signs? T-shirts or pins with a Route 66 image? Models of classic cars—the kind that people drove before the Interstate Highway system made Route 66 itself a relic? All are possible gifts. Other landmarks in New Mexico include Carlsbad Caverns and the Roswell area. Capital Santa Fe is synonymous with Native American arts and crafts, and it is also home to the Georgia O'Keeffe Museum. For those whose taste goes more to food, New Mexican cuisine traditionally means hot and spicy, as in red and green chilies, so give a gastronomic gift featuring these kinds of chilies, and you're sure to please the food lovers you know.

New York

Much of what people think of as being in a New York state of mind comes from the downstate part of the Empire State: fresh bagels and bialys, New York cheesecake, Times Square, Broadway, subway cars, yellow cabs, the Statue of Liberty, and the Brooklyn Bridge. But beyond New York City, the state is also home to Niagara Falls (and all of its touristy trinkets) and many notable colleges and universities: Cornell, Columbia, Culinary Institute of America, Vassar, NYU, and more. The vegetarian in your life will drool over a Moosewood cookbook, based on a popular vegetarian restaurant in Ithaca. New York also makes headlines for its Rome apples and Long Island wine.

North Carolina

What put North Carolina on the map in the minds of many folks was the Wright Brothers' flying machine, which first left the ground at Kitty Hawk—and earned the state the right to put "First in Flight" on the license plate. Turning from the wild blue yonder back to the turf, gift options include merchandise related to the Tar Heels of the University of North Carolina and the other big basketball school down the road from Raleigh—Duke University. Residents and visitors to North Carolina also bask in the state's many natural beauties, the big three being the Outer Banks, the Great Smoky Mountains, and the Blue Ridge Parkway.

North Dakota

Good gifts to choose include items that capture the early history of the Dakotas and any of the wholesome foods made from locally grown ingredients, such as chokecherries, durum wheat, barley, corn, soybeans, and sunflower seeds. Residents of the Sioux State are proud of their Native American heritage, as they are of the North Dakota Museum of Art in Grand Forks—both can help when you need ideas for a gift.

Ohio

Two architectural landmarks in the Buckeye State inspire Ohio-related gifts: the Rock and Roll Hall of Fame and Museum (Cleveland) and the Longaberger Basket Company (Newark). With its I. M. Pei-designed glass triangular structure jutting from the edge of Lake Erie, the Hall of Fame is an imposing sight. Inside, you'll find chart-topping souvenirs to make a music lover happy. Due east of the capital city of Columbus, you can't miss the corporate headquarters of Longaberger: the building is shaped like one of the picnic baskets the company sells. These sturdy beauties are made of high-quality hardwood maples, and each is signed and dated on the bottom by the artisan. Naturally enough, they're a classic collector's item.

Oklahoma

Oklahoma has the largest concentration of Native Americans—about sixty different tribes—of any state, making Native American crafts an outstanding gift to give. Another is material related to native son Will Rogers. Oklahoma, the Sooner State, is also known for some of its baked goods, including products of the Shawnee Milling Company; visit the corporate headquarters in Shawnee for cooking- and baking-related gifts. Another food-related landmark is in Oklahoma City: Famous Mel's Sandwich & Bake Shop; go there to buy mouth-watering cinnamon rolls.

Oregon

The beauty of nature gives Oregon its grandeur—and its residents pride. Oregon is home to the country's deepest lake, Crater Lake, surrounded by dense forests. There's also the rugged Pacific coastline and its awe-inspiring cliffs. Like many other western states, Oregon is a place to be active, whether it be kayaking down the Columbia River or climbing Mount Hood. Put it all together with a gift that embraces the outdoors, and you're sure to find something that's just right for the active person on your gift list. Another memorial of the Beaver State would be anything featuring this official animal. Oregon also produces some diverse foods, including Tillamook cheeses, marionberry jams and jellies, and hazelnuts.

Pennsylvania

The Keystone State is steeped in Colonial and Revolutionary history—from Washington's Crossing of the Delaware to the Liberty Bell—which constitutes a broad category of memorable gifts. Another way to go back in time is via Lancaster County, which is Amish country and thus a repository of Amish-made furniture and crafts. Pennsylvanians are also praised for their food, and the smorgasbord of packaged treats from companies headquartered here includes Hershey candies, Herr's potato chips, and Tastycake snack cakes. You can also walk away with an original Philly cheese steak or Pennsylvania Dutch pretzel. Finally, a souvenir of any of the three P's—Pittsburgh, Philadelphia, and the Poconos—would be a good choice.

Rhode Island

Rhode Island is a tiny state, but there's a lot going on here. To whet your whistle, the Ocean State has two official drinks—lemonade and coffee milk—both of which make refreshing gifts. Rhode Island is also where you'll find the stately mansions of Newport and the origins of the game of lawn tennis. Each year, great tunes flood the Newport Jazz Festival. For food gifts that hit the spot, there's johnnycake meal and Rhode Island quahogs (a shellfish). And toy classic Mr.

Potato Head recently became Rhode Island's unofficial mascot, mostly because the toy's creator, Hasbro, Inc., is headquartered in Providence.

South Carolina

A unique treat from South Carolina is ChocRoaches—semisweet chocolate replicas of the palmetto bug, the "Unofficial State Bird of South Carolina." For a more historical angle on food, pick up books on Low Country cooking from Hoppin' John's, a culinary bookstore in Charleston. Also in Charleston is the annual Spoleto Festival, which brings more dance, music, and culture to the state than residents can handle. Sweet-grass baskets are a pretty local craft to buy. And of course, here in the South, items on the Civil War, which should inspire great gift ideas for any military buffs you know, surround you.

South Dakota

As corny as it may sound, one of the biggest doings in South Dakota is the Corn Palace, a convention center of sorts where locals go for concerts and sporting events. What makes the Corn Palace a novelty is its exterior mural, a tribute to South Dakota agriculture that is constructed of the products it heralds: corn, wheat, wild oats, rye, and more. (The palace itself, though, is made of good old-fashioned building materials and not corn.) Other good gift ideas include books and photos documenting the area's natural and manmade sites, such as the Black Hills, the Badlands, and Mount Rushmore. Since South Dakota is steeped in Native American traditions, items from the Sioux Nation, such as dream catchers and medicine bags, are also laudable.

Tennessee

There is a wide range of music in Tennessee, and anything connected with tune towns such as Memphis (birthplace of the blues) or Nashville (more than one hundred record labels are here) will make a fun gift. You could also focus your gift giving on local attractions such as Dollywood, the Grand Ole Opry, or Graceland, the king of the state's draws. Or look to the Women's Basketball Hall of Fame in Knoxville or the Jack Daniel's Distillery in Lynchburg.

Texas

In the Lone Star State, you'll have a gift recipient dancing the two-step with anything that is Texas-shape, features a cowboy boot, or shows the armadillo (the official small mammal), Texas longhorn (official large mammal), or bluebonnet (official flower). Did you know that the official state dish of Texas is chili? Women called chili queens whipped up the first batches of the mouth-burning stuff in San Antonio some 150 years ago, and it's still beloved by residents and visitors today. Texans are also proud of the part they played in the space missions of yester-year, so the Houston Space Center and its logo items are a continual draw here. If you want to give something big and bright from Texas, go for a Lone Star cut of blue topaz, the state's gem, which creates a single star in the middle of the stone. And of course, there's the omnipresent cowboy hat.

Utah

Two recent happenings that have put Utah on the map (beyond the Osmonds, Brigham Young University, and the Great Salt Lake). They are Robert Redford's Sundance Film Festival and the 2002 Winter Olympics. Both provide great gift ideas. Skiing is world-class here, so perhaps the ski bum in your life would like something from Park City. Utah is the Beehive State, named more for the industriousness of its settlers than a proliferation of honey making. Still, you can run with the idea by choosing an authentic bee skep (a handmade hive, if you will, made of straw or resembling a bee hive) or, in a tamer nature, something made from honey.

Vermont

While Vermont is a state of independent thinkers, where preserving individuals' rights to live as they like is paramount, it is also a place where you can get some really good stuff to eat. Here among the prolific Vermont dairy farms, Ben & Jerry struck ice-cream gold with their eponymous frozen dessert. You can tour the company's factory near Burlington and lick some souvenirs of your own. Likewise, Green Mountain Coffee, which took its name from the state's national forest, delivers an excellent brew. You can also get awesome maple syrup and maple rock candy, and don't forget to pick up a box or two of Lake Champlain chocolates.

Virginia

Dating back as far as Jamestown, Virginia is one of the places that helped get America on its feet, and the state is imbued with history—from the American Revolution to the Civil War. When considering your gift options, you could circle Williamsburg for period costumes and crafts, check out Charlottesville for relics of Thomas Jefferson, and chalk up the cities outside of Washington, D.C.

for a more modern slice of history. On the natural order, there are the shores of Virginia Beach and the peaks of the Blue Ridge and Shenandoah Mountains to look towards for gift ideas.

Washington

For those with an affinity for the Seattle area, products that revolve around the city's Pike Street Market or the Space Needle are crowd pleasers. A gift for out-doorsy types is something from Mount Rainier National Park. Walla Walla onions hail from Washington, as do Washington State apples, and both go down nicely as food gifts. Or salute local talent past and present with media by or about Jimi Hendrix, Kurt Cobain, or Dale Chihuly, a contemporary artist who works in glass and hails from Tacoma. Finally, flag anything with the logo of Redmond-based Microsoft as gifts for techies.

West Virginia

West Virginia is a haven for white-water rafting—especially on the New River in the southern part of the state. The state's ultra-luxurious Greenbrier Hotel is a chic place to purchase pampering gifts. West Virginia is considered the Mountain State because it's home to two mountain ranges: the Appalachians and the Alleghenies. Not surprisingly the state's motto has something to do with mountains, too: "Mountaineers Always Free." This state was forever memorialized in John Denver's song "Take Me Home, Country Roads."

Wisconsin

If you want to make a Wisconsin resident smile, say "cheese." This is America's Dairyland, where the populace proudly refer to themselves as "cheese heads." Give a Green Bay Packers fan a hat shaped like a wedge of cheese, or a University of Wisconsin Badgers follower anything decked with this official state animal, and you'll have made this person very happy. Oshkosh B'Gosh and Lands' End, both of which are headquartered here, are great sources for fashion conscious givers and receivers. For crafts think of Door County, which sticks out into the western shores of Lake Michigan and sometimes is referred to as the Cape Cod of the Midwest.

Wyoming

When you see that bison waving on the Wyoming state flag, you know you've found the perfect icon for a gift. Wyoming is very much a western state, where cowboy gear rules, wagon trains once rolled, and legends such as Buffalo Bill Cody and Calamity Jane once lived. It is also home to Jackson Hole, a popular ski town, and Yellowstone National Park, with its famous geyser Old Faithful. For an authentic food gift, try smoked meats or "Cowboy Coffee," a Jackson Hole java maker.

*   *   *   *   *

How to Write Thank-You Notes

A recurring complaint I get about giving and receiving is this: Why don't people write thank-you notes anymore? I've heard from wedding guests who marveled that the bride and groom never acknowledged their gifts, and business executives who were dismayed that associates didn't take the time to send a handwritten thank-you note after being treated to dinner or sitting through a presentation. Sure, E-mail is speedier and easier, but I'm a stickler for certain social rules, and writing a brief but heartfelt (and handwritten) note to acknowledge a gift, a meeting, or plain old hospitality is fundamental.

While my mother drilled me early on about the whys and hows of the thank-you note—and I'm passing that instruction along to my daughters—I've come to realize that one reason so many people don't send thank-you notes has nothing to do with being rude, ungrateful, or lazy. Rather, it's because they were never taught *how* to do it, so they're intimidated by the prospect—and they let that fear paralyze them into doing nothing.

If you happen to be among those citizens for whom composing a thank-you note doesn't come naturally, these concluding pointers will have you writing these notes in no time.

Invest in Nice Stationery or Notepaper

First and foremost, you can't prepare to write a notable note without nice stationery or notepaper on which to write. Just as I stock up on all-occasion gifts for my gift closet, I keep a supply of notepaper on hand that I can use for my personal correspondence as well. I sometimes buy cards on sale that actually say "Thank you" on the front, but just as often, I buy generic cards that I like and that would be suitable for writing a thank-you note. When I get a gift unexpectedly, I don't have to make a special trip to the store or make do with a sheet from a legal pad to thank the person.

Get Organized

If you're the guest of honor at an event, or any time you'll be receiving a large number of gifts in a short period of time—such as at a bridal shower, a birthday party, or even Christmas—it's critical to keep a running list of who gave you what. Jot down the name of the giver, the specific gift, and any brief positive thoughts or feelings that jump into your head as you open it. This list will help you in two ways: it will prevent you from forgetting anyone when you write out your thank-you notes (crossing off the names as I go gives me an added sense of accomplishment), and incorporating the thoughts you'd originally recorded about each gift lets you personalize the message.

Log Off: It Must Be Handwritten

I know how easy it would be to cut-and-paste some quickie thank-you notes in a word processing program or an E-mail message, but a computer-generated note just doesn't have the same effect as a handwritten one nor should you ever substitute it for the old-fashioned kind. So, always take the time to write it longhand.

If you're helping a young child send a thank-you note, write the body yourself as you recite it out loud together, and then have the child "sign" his or her name. Don't worry if the letters in the signature are backwards or out of order. The fact that she personally signed it will mean more than you know to the gift giver who receives this missive in the mail.

Don't Overdo It

Here's a simple formula for writing a thank-you note that is personal, filled with emotion, and yet succinct:

1. Start by thanking the person for the specific gift. Begin by saying, "Dear Ginger: Thank you so much for the matched set of hats, gloves, and scarf" or "Dear Fred: Thank you for your generous check." When you identify the gift right up front, you're telling the giver that conveying personal thanks is important to you and that you're not just sending out generic thank-yous as a timesaver. Remember: the giver devoted time, thought, and money to you and your gift; you owe it to that person to at least write out a few phrases of gratitude.

2. Mention how you'll use the gift. In your next sentence, write something like "This set of winter accessories will keep me snug when I go outside to play with my kids." You want to communicate exactly how you'll be able to put the gift to use and why it's so perfect for your lifestyle. If you've received a gift of cash, explain what you hope to do with the money—even if it's just depositing it in a savings account for college. Say something like "I plan to use your check to help buy books at college" or "I'm going to use it to treat myself to a manicure."

3. Thank the giver again and finish the note. All you need to do is write one more line to say something like "Thanks again for the great gift and for remembering my birthday" and you're home free. Sign your name, and congratulate yourself for having just written a thank-you note with impressive style. Of course, if you want to add a few more lines before you sign, seal, and deliver it, that's OK, too.

4. Proofread your note before sending it. I can't tell you how many times I've written a thank-you note and put *your* for *you're* or made a similar mistake. Thank goodness I proof everything before I mail it. If you spot a mistake in your handiwork, fix it. You can write the correction right on the note or, if you're feeling so inclined and you have enough stationery on hand, write the note over again. Tip: Be extra careful *not* to make the same error again. If you do rewrite, proofread the second version too, just to be sure.

What to Do About Gifts You Don't Like

You may wonder what you're supposed to do about thank-you notes when you don't really like a gift you've received. I don't care if you return it to the store, give it to charity, or put it up for sale on eBay—you still need to thank the gift giver. In this case, your second line of the thank-you note should focus on some redeeming quality of the gift, however small. For example, if someone gave you an ugly crystal duck, you could say something like "I love how sparkly the crystal gets when the sun hits it." Or, if someone gave you clothing that doesn't fit, isn't your color, or you would just never wear, say something like "I love the clothes from store X," which lets you get away with expressing your enthusiasm for the effort while making no mention per se of the article in question. If you can't find anything positive to say, at least attempt to offer a compliment to the gift giver: "It was one of the most creative gifts we received." The ideal here is to accomplish the task of thanking the giver without having to choke down any lies.

Time Is of the Essence

Now for the most important guideline: Regardless of what stationery you use or which adjective you choose to describe your gratitude, make sure you send your thank-you note within two weeks of receiving a gift. You'll be long remembered for your thoughtfulness.

APPENDIX

I've gathered contact information for the companies and products I've mentioned in the book, in case you're interested in checking out some of them:

1-800-FLOWERS
www.1800flowers.com

Ann Taylor
www.anntaylor.com
(800) DIAL-ANN (342-5266)

All About Baby
"Babyography"
www.allbaby.com
(805) 373-5197

Amazon.com
www.amazon.com

Banana Republic
www.bananarepublic.com

Barnes and Noble
www.barnesandnoble.com

Bed, Bath & Beyond
www.bedbathandbeyond.com
(800) GO BEYOND (462-3966)

Berea College Crafts
www.berea.com

Best Buy
www.bestbuy.com

BizRate.com
www.bizrate.com

Blockbuster
www.blockbuster.com

Chaddsford Winery
www.chaddsford.com
(610) 388-6221

Coach
www.coach.com
(888) 262-6224

Consumer Products Safety Commission
www.cpsc.gov

"Cookie Bouquet"
Cookies by Design
www.cookiesbydesign.com

Crate & Barrel
www.crateandbarrel.com
(800) 967-6696

Eastern Mountain Sports (EMS)
www.ems.com
(888) 463-6367

eBay
www.ebay.com

Gap
www.gap.com
(800) GAPSTYLE (427-7895)

Georgette Klinger
www.georgetteklinger.com
(800) KLINGER (554-6437)

Godiva
www.godiva.com
(800) 9 GODIVA (946-3482)

Gymboree
www.gymboree.com

Harry and David
www.harryanddavid.com
(877) 322-1200

Heifer Project International
www.heifer.org
(800) 422-0474

Hershey Chocolate Factory Tours
http://www.hersheys.com/discover/chocolate.asp

Jelly Belly Jelly Beans Factory Tours
www.jellybelly.com

Jos A. Banks
www.josabank.com

Le Creuset
www.lecreuset.com

Lenox Gift Company
www.lenox.com

Linens 'n Things
www.lnt.com
(866) 568-7378

L.L. Bean
www.llbean.com
(800) 441-5713

Louis Vuitton
www.vuitton.com

Lowe's
www.lowes.com

Marshall's
www.marshallsonline.com

Metropolitan Museum of Art store
http://www.metmuseum.org/store/index.asp
(800) 468-7386

Montblanc
http://www.worldlux.com/montblanc-pens.html
(888) 721-7367

Name Train
Maple Landmark
www.maplelandmark.com
(800) 421-4223

National Arbor Day Foundation
www.arborday.org
(888) 448-7337

National Safe Kids Campaign
www.safekids.org

Neiman Marcus
www.neimanmarcus.com

New Hope Winery
www.newhopewinery.com
(800) 592-WINE (9463)

Nordstrom
www.nordstrom.com
(888) 282-6060

Office Depot
www.officedepot.com

Pier One
www.pier1.com

Pottery Barn
www.potterybarn.com
(888) 779-5176

Radio Shack
www.radioshack.com

Rain Forest Rescue
www.rainforestrescue.org

REI
www.rei.com

Ross-Simons catalog
www.ross-simons.com
(800) 458-4545

Runner's World
www.runnersworld.com

Saks Fifth Avenue
www.saksfifthavenue.com
(877) 551-SAKS (7257)

Signals Catalog
www.signals.com
(800) 669-9696

Southern Living at Home
www.southernlivingathome.com

SpaFinders
www.spafinders.com
(800) ALL-SPAS (255-7727)

SpaWish
www.spawish.com
(888) SPA-WISH (772-9474)

Staples
www.staples.com
(800) 3STAPLE (378-2753)

Steuben
www.steuben.com

Target
www.target.com

The Home Depot
www.homedepot.com

Tiffany & Company
www.tiffany.com

TJ Maxx
www.tjmaxx.com

Toys R Us
www.toysrus.com

Tower Records
www.towerrecords.com
(800) ASK TOWER (275-8693)

Watch It Made in the U.S.A.
www.factorytour.com

Waterford
www.waterford.com

Waterman
www.waterman.com

Williams-Sonoma
www.williams-sonoma.com
(877) 812-6235

Windsor Vineyards
www.windsorvineyards.com
(800) 333-9987

INDEX

A

B

C

Consumer Products Safety Commission, 25, 67, 128
Copper (as an anniversary gift), 34-35
Coral (as an anniversary gift), 40
Corn Palace, 120
Cornell University, 117
Cotton (as an anniversary gift), 30-31
Cowboy Coffee, 123
Crate & Barrel, 53, 96-97, 128
Crystal or Glass
    As an anniversary gift, 31, 39
    As a business gift, 58
Culinary Institute of America, 117

D

Dale Chihuly, 122
Dave Barry, 112
David Letterman, 113
Delaware, Gifts from or about, 111
Denver, Colorado, 111
Desk Sets (as an anniversary gift), 34-35
Diamond (as an anniversary gift), 36,40
Diamond Anniversary, 40
Diamond Jewelry, 36, 40
District of Columbia, Gifts from or about, 111-112
Dollywood, 120
Duke University, 118
Dupont, 111

E

Eastern Mountain Sports (EMS) 96
eBay, 5, 8, 29, 36, 47-48, 97, 102, 104-105, 112, 125, 129, 135
Electrical Appliances (as an anniversary gift), 31-32
Elvis Presley, 115
Emerald (as an anniversary gift), 40
Eskimo, 110
Ethel M Chocolates, 116

F

K

L

O

P

Q

R

T

Tabasco, 114
Tastycake, 119
Target, 7, 19, 46, 47, 49, 64, 70, 132
Tennessee, Gifts from or about, 120
Tennessee Williams, 115
Texas, Gifts from or about, 120-121
Textiles (as an anniversary gift), 38
Thank You Notes
    How to write, 123-126
    When to send 126
The Best Gift I Ever Gave, 6, 15, 17, 22, 42-44, 46-47, 49, 52, 61, 66-67, 78
The Best Gift I Ever Got, 5, 13-14, 18, 23-24, 34, 42, 45, 47, 49, 54, 56, 63-64, 68-69, 76, 81
The Complete Guide for the Anxious Bride, 9
The Complete Guide for the Anxious Groom, 93
The Wizard of Oz, 113
Thomas Edison, 117
Tiffany & Company, 51, 132
Times Square, 33, 117
Titanic, 111
Timepiece
    As an anniversary gift, 31, 39
    When not to give, 55
Tin (as an anniversary gift), 36
Tin Cup, 36
Tin Men, 36
Tipping
    At holidays, 72-73
Tom Petty, 112
Toys R Us, 46, 70, 132
Tower Records, 47, 70, 132
Travel, as a gift, 39, 83
Tree-Trimming, Gifts for, 70-71

U

UFOs
    Area 51, 116

X

Y

About The Author

Leah Ingram is the author of nine books: *The Everything Etiquette Book: Second Edition* (Adams Media, 2005); *Buying & Selling Your Way to a Fabulous Wedding with eBay* (Thomson, 2004); *Plan Your Wedding In No Time* (QUE Publishing, 2004); *The Complete Guide for the Anxious Bride* (New Pages Books, 2004); *The Balanced Bride: Preparing Your Mind, Body, and Spirit for Your Wedding and Beyond* (Contemporary Books/McGraw-Hill, 2002); *You Shouldn't Have! How to Give Gifts They'll Love* (Contemporary Books/McGraw-Hill, 2001); *Your Wedding Your Way* (Contemporary Books, 2000); *The Portable Wedding Consultant* (Contemporary Books, 1997); and *The Bridal Registry Book* (Contemporary Books, 1995).

Ingram is a media-savvy author who has made more than 200 appearances on local and national television to talk about wedding planning and gift giving for various occasions. Much of Ingram's exposure to the media has been in her role as a spokesperson, where she is a sought-after personality. She has completed television and radio tours for national companies like 1800-Flowers.com, Bath and Body Works, VISA Gift Cards, BlueNile.com and many others.

Ingram is also a frequently quoted wedding, gift and etiquette authority. Recent stories in The New York Times, The Wall Street Journal, The Philadelphia Inquirer, The Christian Science Monitor and Modern Bride have included her words of wisdom.

In addition, she is a certified etiquette and protocol consultant, as well as an accomplished journalist. She writes frequently about shopping, weddings, entertaining and gift giving. Her byline has appeared in many well-known publications including Allure, Parade Magazine, Family Circle, Woman's Day, Bridal Guide, Islands, New York, The New York Times and USA Weekend.

978-0-595-33621-0
0-595-33621-3

Printed in the United States
65629LVS00004B/334